THE
CUSTOMER
SUCCESS
PIONEER

THE CUSTOMER SUCCESS PIONEER

THE FIRST 12 MONTHS OF YOUR JOURNEY INTO GROWTH

KELLIE LUCAS

First published in Great Britain by Practical Inspiration Publishing, 2019

© Kellie Lucas, 2019

The moral rights of the author have been asserted

ISBN   978-1-78860-039-2
       978-1-78860-038-5 (mobi)
       978-1-78860-040-8 (epub)

Every effort has been made to trace copyright holders and to obtain their permission for the use of copyright material. The publisher apologises for any errors or omissions and would be grateful if notified of any corrections that should be incorporated in future reprints or editions of this book.

Practical Inspiration
PUBLISHING

Praise for *The Customer Success Pioneer*

The Customer Success Pioneer covers the foundational topics of establishing your Customer Success organisation. It provides insight into why this is an accelerating business imperative and practical guidance of how to create and evolve your customer-focused activities, including how to align this across your entire business and why you should! It is the perfect complement to Customer Success - How Innovative Companies Are Reducing Churn and Growing Recurring Revenue. I'm thankful to Kellie for writing this book as it needed to come from someone with extensive and "dirty hands" experience like her. Authors of Customer Success books cannot live in ivory towers. *Dan Steinman: General Manager, Gainsight EMEA and Co-Author "Customer Success - How Innovative Companies..."*

A highly informative book loaded with practical and proven customer success advice drawn from Kellie's many years of experience. An absolute must for any executive looking to design their customer success program. *Irit Eizips: Chief Customer Officer and CEO, CSM Practice and Top 100 Customer Success Strategist 2013-2018*

Perhaps the most vital attribute of a Customer Success Manager is domain expertise sufficient to enable a person to speak with "the voice of authority." Possession of such knowledge is a key factor in becoming a trusted advisor. In her book, *The Customer Success Pioneer*, Kellie Lucas clearly demonstrates deep domain expertise in the profession of Customer Success Management. Using her DIME approach, Design, Implement, Measure and Evolve, Kellie takes her audience through the tasks and realizations that ought to be accomplished during the initial 12 months of a Customer Success Initiative in any company.

Yes, you can Do It Yourself — many CS professionals have done so in companies all around the world for many years now. *The Customer Success Pioneer* provides you with a clear map of the journey to be undertaken. Used properly, the book will save you substantial amounts of time and money, and vastly increase your chances for success in your initiative. *Mikael Blaisdell: Executive Director, The Customer Success Association and The Customer Success Forum*

Kellie is one of the most admired thought-leaders in the Customer Success space and whose opinion I respect greatly. Her excellent book provides an invaluable insight into the importance of Customer Success and how it can make meaningful differences to all businesses who truly care about helping their clients realise maximum ROI. Not only will this book help you to develop a Customer Success framework, it will also provide the guidance you need to ensure that it evolves with your business and that you are able to measure its effectiveness – both internally and externally. *Adam Joseph: Founder, CSM Insight and Director of Customer Success, Gainsight EMEA*

The Customer Success Pioneer is a masterful cookbook for anyone seriously considering setting up a Customer Success organisation or designing the next stage of its evolution. Read this book - and don't forget to take notes! *Rohit George: Regional Vice President - Customer Success, MuleSoft*

With the rapid shift towards recurring revenue and subscription-based business models, Customer Success is now vital to the health of so many organisations. Whether just getting started in Customer Success or a seasoned Customer Success professional this book is invaluable in helping develop and imbed the culture of Customer Success within your organisation. Kellie has brought together key organisational structures, methodologies and metrics to support the development of a Customer Success organisation that can become a revenue growth engine for your business. *James Russell: Senior Manager, Client Success EMEA, Bazaarvoice and Customer Success Leader and Strategist*

The elements involved in building and running a successful Customer Success programme are often underestimated, and as there are no One Size Fits All solutions it can be a tricky area to cover in a book like this. *The Customer Success Pioneer* addresses this by breaking down a series of potentially complex topics into bite-sized chunks, highlighting the small things you should be thinking about when you set up a CSM programme, whilst making you aware of the bigger things you could be aiming for in the future. It isn't intended to do your thinking for you and it will definitely make you think. I wish I had this book ten years ago! *Mike Blackadder: Chief Customer Officer, Artesian.co*

At Artesian we were lucky enough to attract Dr Steve Garnett as an angel investor; as EMEA Chairman of Salesforce.com his guidance was clear and we were never in any doubt about the subscription model we would build our sales acceleration technology around. Every SaaS company is up for re-election every year or two and so as critical as building great products and acquiring the customers you want, helping them succeed and continually quantify the benefit your software is deriving is mission critical. Kellie was instrumental in helping our company scale and grow. She will remember I asked her to build our 'happiness engineering department' - a mantra she embraced. After Kellie left our company we continued that great work and today we are proud to say we hit those magical gross and net retention numbers every year with happy customers who can talk to and measure great results.

What you will see in this book is that journey and Kellie's learning. A must read for every SaaS business leader. *Andrew Yates: CEO & Founder, Artesian.co*

Being in a Customer Success role can be daunting. So many people still asking, "what do you do and how do you do it?" There's pressure to understand customers, decrease churn and grow revenue. If you, like many, don't know where to start, then *The Customer Success Pioneer* is a must read. Not only a great reset on what Customer Success is and what we want to achieve but more importantly how to achieve it. Practical steps to set up, empower and measure a Customer Success team in your organisation. Join the pioneers and have an impact in your role! *Ian Sloan: VP of Customer Success, Avvio*

The Customer Success Pioneer is a great read for anyone trying to plan their journey into the challenging world of launching a customer success practice. It provides an extremely clear, comprehensive and logical path for identifying, understanding and addressing all the organizational challenges and complexities required to launch a high-impact customer success program. I highly recommend this book. *Jason Whitehead: CEO, Tri Tuns and Co-Founder, CSMastermind*

Still scratching your head and unsure where to start? - then stop. The 'new' philosophy and profession of Customer Success is here to stay and you need to read this book today; follow the DIME framework and get onboard the subscription economy train to understand why your customers now need to be for life not just a sales transaction. Get that right and you will tap into your company's biggest growth engine - your existing customer base! Evolving into a SaaS business? Then get a copy of this manual and become a CS Pioneer yourself! Starting with the origins, the roots, the history, the current state and everything in between since the late 90s - this book covers it all and really will be "your constant companion" as you evolve and grow through your customer success journey. You will learn why for so long we really didn't understand or practice the misunderstood term of "customer is king". *Amanjit Sandhu: Director EMEA Customer Success, Cloud & Support, JDA Software*

With Kellie's many years' experience in Customer Success and leadership this book allows you to tap into all her practical learnings. This is a great alternative to the other CS-related books on the market and will support both the novice CS practioner and the seasoned, experienced CS leader. What I find most valuable in this book is not just the "how" but the "why"; the context of customer success in a SaaS business. Give yourself the best chance of being successful by reading this book and applying the large volume of sound advice Kellie provides! **Matt Myszkowski: VP Customer Success Management, SAP**

If you have been lucky enough to work with Kellie or learn from her numerous speaking engagements and workshops at Customer Success events, you can imagine the value this book can provide. *The Customer Success Pioneer* will provide you with the tools and framework to start a sustainable CSM programme. **Steven Lewandowski: Director Global Customer Success, Signavio**

The Customer Success Pioneer is a pragmatic book about the role of customer success, which is taking the business world by storm. Customer success leaders and practitioners of today are indeed pioneers, paving the path for an even greater customer success journey in years to come. In reference to the subtitle "…your journey into growth", this book reads like a GPS, guiding the reader with digestible and hands-on directions of what to do and where, whilst setting out on their initial customer success journey.

The Northern Star is the DIME methodology which provides the iterative roadmap for the initiation and implementation of a customer success organisation. The content is practical, well-structured and provides nuggets of hands-on tips and tricks at the end of each section. This is a must-have handbook for customer success professionals to read, re-read and consult all along their iterative customer success journeys, irrespective of whether it's the first 12 months or beyond. As pioneers of customer success, we've all got plenty of room to grow. **Sue Nabeth Moore: Founder, Success Track Enterprise and Co-Founder, CSMastermind and Customer Success Outcomes**

Never has a new function in an organisation enjoyed such attention and dynamic growth as Customer Success and that brings with it added scrutiny and the expectation to deliver maximum impact in the shortest time. That is where *The Customer Success Pioneer* becomes a must-use guide for organisations that want to maximize their return on Customer Success. It brilliantly demystifies the Customer Success role, judiciously positioning Customer Success as the critical customer facing role to truly serve the customer's needs. The book provides a practical step by step approach to the practitioners of Customer Success, both new and tenured. Industry best practices are distilled into usable real-world frameworks that can be easily followed and implemented. Kellie's winning formula is that she educates and empowers the reader to take their own stand on Customer Success while "ideas are forming and transforming on a regular basis". **Kay Mukherjee: Head of Customer Success EMEA at Splunk**

To you,
my fellow Customer Success pioneer.
Explore, branch out, grow.
Be extraordinary...

Contents

List of figures

Acknowledgements

The seeds were sown for this book in my hometown of Winneba, Ghana, during my time with Challenging Heights (www.challengingheights.org). It was entirely fitting, therefore, that the final edits to the delivery draft were completed while sitting with my exceptional team there, on a return visit earlier this year. I am eternally grateful for my team, their support and encouragement and their never-ending dedication to their community and the direct beneficiaries of their invaluable programming, in the fight against child trafficking and slavery. I am also grateful to LJ for giving me "oftentimes".

The seeds were nurtured and grown into a fully-fledged "being" in many locations as I've bounced between Spain, Ghana, Singapore, London and Dorset over the last couple of years. I thank Cheryl for giving me the space to inch my way through the early chapters, Leah and Raj for the fabulous balcony office in Singapore and Aden for only distracting me in the afternoons for playtime! I especially thank David and Sarah for cracking the whip to get me across the finishing line for the first draft; DIME would never have been born without your tenacity and support.

Special thanks are also due to Dave and Annie, without whom the pioneer spirit would never have been born. The two of you truly helped me work through some gritty early thought processes with confidence and grace and fed me Christmas punch while pushing towards the first draft finish line!

Artesian gave me the opportunity to practice what I preach, so I thank Andrew and Mike for trusting and backing me to build a solid and best in practice Customer Success function. Without them, this book may never have seen the light of day.

Thanks also go to Mike and Dale for being so enthusiastic and encouraging when I mentioned that I might write a book. Special thanks to Dale for always knowing the right thing to say at the exact right time and making a mercy dash to keep me going, when it was most needed. You see me, you hear me. Thank you.

Dan and Karen Steinman for supporting me in so many ways on my journey through Customer Success, to Ghana and back again and I'm sure, into the future.

Sue Nabeth Moore for encouraging me every step of the way and for being the first to publicise the advent of the book, long before there was even a complete draft!

All my friends and family for putting up with me through this insanely emotional and steep learning curve. I will try to make it up to you, somehow, someday.

A special mention is also reserved for my sister-cousin, Jane, for providing the bottle of bubbles with which I celebrated finishing my first full draft!

Finally, I would like to send full appreciation to Alison Jones, who is a wonderful coach and publisher, and her entire team at Practical Inspiration Publishing, who have walked me through the process, every step of the way, with supreme calm, patience and understanding. Thank you.

Foreword

A key premise of this book – that it manifests a pioneering spirit – struck me as nothing short of inspired when I first heard it. After all, a flourishing subscription economy and the rapidly growing field of Customer Success management required pioneers to lay the foundations that carried us this far.

Customer Success, as a discipline, is being defined, at least in part, by the many successful and growing on-demand companies such as ServiceNow, Workday, Hubspot and Zendesk. Whilst they are themselves innovators, few would deny the debt they owe to Marc Benioff and Parker Harris who, in the late 1990s, started the Salesforce business on the notion that systems could be delivered to customers without taking delivery of either hardware or software.

During one of my early consulting assignments, the CIO pointed proudly at a picture on his office wall of their new hard drives being delivered. They were being lifted into the building by crane. Windows had been removed and the main road into town had been temporarily closed in preparation. Two drives, each a gigabyte in storage, a little on the small size for an SD card now, had literally stopped the traffic. Software functionality, without the need for a single line of code, known as software as a service (SaaS) was itself built on innovation that has made such anecdotes historical curiosities. Werner Vogels and Chris Pinkham of Amazon Web Services, Jonathan Bryce of Rackspace, Urs Holzle of Google and many more made potentially unlimited computing capacity available through little more than a web browser, and certainly without cranes.

This shift from owning to subscribing is not just electronic. Whilst digital distribution from the likes of Netflix and Spotify are perfect for such a model, there are a growing number of businesses that provide physical products. Michelle Phan, an American YouTube personality, allows her customers to subscribe to cosmetics through Ipsy, a company she founded with Marcello Camberos and Jennifer Jaconetti Goldfarb. Berlin-based HelloFresh – started by Dominik Richter, Thomas Griesel and Jessica Nilsson – prepares and provides the ingredients needed for those that then enjoy the last thirty minutes of a cooking experience. Indeed, the idea borrows from the 1950s Betty Crocker brand. General Mills, the brand owner, discovered that sales of their cake mixes soared when they left out dried egg and required a fresh egg to be added. Busy consumers need convenience but they also still want to be invested in the food they put on the table.

And there are many more: subscription grooming from Dollar Shave, car-sharing from Zipcar, and new players coming to the market every year. Each of these ground-breaking companies has one thing in common. Their focus has moved from transacting to interacting. Customers have not made long-term, perpetual commitments to them. Rather their clients pledge their patronage for a period of time, after which they will consider continuing. This fundamentally changes the relationship dynamics. Now the supplier cannot rest once they have wooed with promises and sweet nothings whispered as customers progress through their marketing funnel. Instead, the funnel is extended. The supplier must continue to impress.

They must constantly refresh their commitments if the customer is to remain in the relationship. Perhaps, in those early days, Benioff and Parker completely understood where this was going. More likely it is what twentieth-century sociologist Robert K. Merton popularised as *unintended consequence*. In any case, the growth of these businesses is dependent on reciprocal customer relationships not just shipping products. Subscription companies live and die by their ability to continually delight their customers.

Phan, Vogels, Richter and their companies are deserving of our respect. They venture into the unknown, re-write rules and do so without precedents and safety nets, and often without the understanding or support of the incumbent group. Benioff could not fund Salesforce with conventional financing because every Silicon Valley investor turned him down. Not a single indigenous venture capitalist dollar went into kick-starting the subscription revolution.

Customer Success managers, leaders and teams are today's pioneers. Their beginnings are characterised by justification, usually an economic one, that they should even exist at all. In traditional businesses, support specialists deal with cases, implementation consultants are measured in terms of utilisation and Account Managers live or die by a quota. By contrast, few are confident enough to write Customer Success Manager job specifications or compensation plans from scratch.

It isn't uncharted territory anymore, nor is it embryonic, but it is still changing and rapidly so. Established teams find they need to continually reinvent themselves as the impact of putting the customer at the core of a business changes it from the inside out. Working in such close customer proximity is right – indeed, there is no longer any other sustainable option, but it is not the easiest route. Rather, it's a transformational journey requiring constant course corrections. The reverberations are felt by Product, by Sales, indeed every function all collaborating with the Customer Success team and expecting their leadership as the business adapts and grows.

The Customer Success Pioneer then is a beginning but it is, by necessity, much more than that. Whilst encouragement for the pioneer is essential when building out and implementing those thirty, sixty- and ninety-day plans, it does not stop after the first twelve or even twenty-four months. Customer Success forerunners will need help getting past firefighting, beyond the need to curtail churn and into the realms of operational advocacy.

Your team may have just formed or you might be two years in. You may be putting out fires or proactively leading your customers through increasing levels of value. In either case the job at hand is still really pioneering. This book is your constant companion. It will set you off in the right direction and prepare you for each stage of your growth. You will be thankful for having it at your side. As will your customers. Both parties at the vendor and client side of a SaaS relationship are in a new, progressive and emerging relationship in which success is mutual.

Dale Roberts

I

WELCOME TO YOUR JOURNEY

1
WELCOME TO
YOUR JOURNEY

Customer Success is...?

Customer Success is quite simply a business imperative to truly, consistently and perpetually know and *understand* your customers.

You may be confused and feel that this concept is already well known and adopted by businesses and indeed has been for many decades. After all, hasn't the phrase 'Customer is King' been around for, like, forever?

This is true. We have paid lip service, for a very long time, to saying that the customer is always right and that we must be 'customer-centric'. I have known many businesses who have this as one of their business values.

However, do we truly embody the practice or are we just creating the 'spin' required to fool customers into thinking we really care? In reality, our own profit margin and cost reduction exercises have always been the highest priority.

With the transition from perpetual licence to subscriptions (see below), the technology world can no longer afford to be blasé about this topic.

 It is literally life or death for your business, if you are not fully and demonstrably committed to knowing and understanding your customer. Return on Investment (RoI) has also been crowned as being king and for your customers;

this is absolutely a key objective. It is imperative you can support the delivery of their business objectives and prove your contribution to them and their RoI.

In a business economy where customers have freedom of movement more than ever before, the urgency for embracing Customer Success is a reality.

> Nothing is more important to Salesforce than customer success ... And that's why I believe being so committed to the customer is more important than it's ever been ... because it's really this culture that's driving us forward.
>
> *Marc Benioff, CEO, Salesforce*

This is the reason that the specific discipline and category of Customer Success has been created. It is also the reason that it is under the glare of a bright spotlight and is one of the fastest growing career opportunities.

The power has truly shifted from the vendor to the customer. This is the case for Business to Business (B2B) and Business to Consumer (B2C) and across all industries.

Customers demand results and if they are not happy, they can and will move their business elsewhere at a moment's notice.

There are no more lifetime tie-ins brought about by hefty cancellation penalties or seriously large upfront capital expenditure.

No longer can the vendor blot the ink dry on a contract and then walk away without giving the customer another glance.

We have to support them, we have to care and we have to deliver business objectives.

Again, you may feel that each function within a business already has a handle on this, but isn't it true that we're all working in silos, focused on our task and our responsibility?

Who is working across all of those functions to ensure there is collaboration, alignment, consistency and a focus on ensuring that everything being done has the customer front of mind?

The answer is the Customer Success team and the Chief Customer Officer (CCO).

Origin stories

Customer Success has its roots in the SaaS world (see below). Think of all the services which are delivered via the internet these days – Box, MS Office365, G-Suite, Slack, Survey Monkey, Dropbox, Trello, etc. All of these are software, delivered remotely as a service. Some are free, some always paid for or where premium offerings are paid for, via subscription – consider Amazon Prime, Netflix, Spotify, etc.

What is Software (or anything) as a Service?

In the good old days of Information Technology when hardware was prohibitively expensive and the internet and 'cloud' didn't exist, IT companies made the majority of their income from the sale of the hardware and software alone. This would be paid upfront, as capital expenditure.

The subscription element existed as a comparatively low value (and mandatory) annual support and maintenance contract. If you opted out of this payment, you would forfeit your right to any vendor-provided support and would not receive any product update releases.

The customer took on all the capital expense and the risk of the transaction, the project and the ongoing administration:

- Hardware capital expenditure
- Software capital expenditure
- Annual maintenance and support contract
- Hardware maintenance costs
- Project implementation costs and responsibility
- Perpetual administration

For even the smallest of projects and companies, this undertaking would cost thousands, hundreds of thousands or even millions as an upfront, non-refundable investment.

The vendor rubbed their hands with glee before the ink was dry as they walked away with no responsibilities. Even if their software didn't perform terribly well or even as sold, the supplier was under no obligation to resolve the problems. If you hadn't purchased the annual maintenance and support, then the provider had no responsibility to support you as you weren't using the 'supported version'.

The customer would be dissatisfied and no doubt a detractor but no one cared as the supplier had already received all the income upfront and the customer was stuck with their investment.

See also 3.2 Customer Health (Net Promoter Score)

As the customer would be expecting and tracking a project RoI, they would need to wait at least until the original expenditure had been depreciated in accounting terms to a nil/residual value.

For such a large and costly project, this would generally be over at least ten years. Then and only then, could the customer consider walking away and try to find a more suitable alternative solution.

Often, customers would be so entrenched in the process which had been implemented, the cost of re-engineering was prohibitive, so they stayed locked into the original project and therefore, supplier.

Due to this financial lock-in, vendors were able to make a sale, get the contract signed and then effectively walk away. They didn't need to worry about customer satisfaction or loyalty as those who had signed on the dotted line were already trapped. Advocacy and case studies have always been helpful sales tools but in a world of customer naivety and reliance on the salesperson as the subject matter expert, they were much less valuable or needed. In addition, there were many fewer channels through which to broadcast your dissatisfaction so bad reviews travelled slowly.

The tables turned with the advent of the internet. Communication and education became much easier for everyone. Sales teams were no longer the 'experts' to whom we turned to understand technology, processes and projects.

Customers started to educate themselves with the information which flooded the internet, communicated more easily with their network through email, networking sites such as LinkedIn and social media, and ultimately demanded more from their suppliers.

The advent of the 'cloud' and vastly reduced cost of hardware and data storage meant companies were able to absorb the cost of storing the software and your data on their own servers. This created a flood of entrepreneurial and trend-setting companies who inundated the market with Apps which were free to use and gave the consumer the flexibility to use and discard at their own will and whim. This, in turn, led to the subscription economy: these companies realised they needed to monetise their Apps and software so premium services were offered to encourage users to upgrade and pay for the software.

This created a mindset in us all that we should be able to pick and choose where we spent our time in technology and even more so, have flexibility when it came to our business spending. Ultimately, the purchasers in a B2B relationship forced traditional companies to re-consider how they delivered their technology.

To begin with, traditional companies continued to deliver on-premise (where the purchaser bought all the hardware and software and took all the risk) and it was the more entrepreneurial, new start-up businesses which embraced the SaaS model (where the customer takes none of the risk and all of the control as they can walk away after a very short, if any, notice period).

	Perpetual licence	SaaS
On-premise	Almost always	Almost never
Cloud-based	Almost never	Almost always
Capital expenditure	Upfront and high cost	n/a
Subscription	Almost never	Yes
Customer locked-in	Yes	Short-term contract
Risk	Customer	Vendor
Reward	Vendor	Customer
Flexibility	Vendor	Customer
Responsibility	Customer	Vendor
Annual support and maintenance	Mandatory	n/a
Contract length	Long term	Short term
Proof of RoI	Customer	Vendor

Relationship Management	n/a	Critical
Loyalty and advocacy	n/a	Critical
Referenceability	Optional	Mandatory

Figure 0.1: Perpetual licence vs SaaS

One of the earliest adopters and indeed forerunners of the SaaS companies was Salesforce, who supply a CRM (Customer Relationship Management) technology service, within the cloud and therefore as a service.

And so, we circle back to the origin story...

There is a majority consensus which believes the modern birth of Customer Success should be attributed to Salesforce who were early pioneers themselves in the subscription model. They were one of the first companies to offer their software as a service.

In 2005, there was Good News and Bad News at Salesforce. The good news was that the company was acquiring new customers at a stunning rate. The Bad News: customers were churning in horrific numbers. Like Bruce Cleveland (Siebel: see below) before them, Salesforce's executive team quickly realized that bringing in new customers couldn't be the end of the story, that there was no way to add enough new customers to survive if they were leaving in greater numbers.

> Salesforce didn't invent Customer Success as a new profession, but the company quickly built what was then the largest CS department in the industry. The group was (and still is) called Customers For Life, and while it was not responsible for renewals, up-sells or cross-sells, it was specifically chartered to address customer retention by increasing user adoption.
>
> *Mikael Blaisdell, Founder, The Customer Success Association, Customer Success analyst and advisor*

Through Mikael's research, he has established that the first department with the label of Customer Success was also a CRM technology company. They were a traditional on-premise company but with a target of 100% referenceable customers, so they understood the importance of successful implementations and knew that, ultimately, customers would drive higher long-term revenue. This introduces us to my golden mantra of Their Success = Your Success.

This occurred in 1996/7, almost exactly a decade before the much publicised Salesforce.com story occurred in 2006.

In addition, chronologically, Siebel was the first on-demand business to recognise the need for a post-sales team to concentrate on retaining and expanding their signed customer base through ensuring they were gaining value and success from the service. In 2005, Bruce Cleveland established and labelled his requisite department, Customer Success management with a mission to increase usage, help customers be successful so that they would remain loyal, remain with the company and expand their contract.

To be or not to be, that is the question

There should be no such question or hesitation. Customer Success should and must permeate all activities undertaken by your entire business, no matter the size or maturity.

The 'new' philosophy and profession of Customer Success is here to stay and many people are still scratching their heads over the concept or are yet to catch up with the frontrunners to even understand that this imperative exists in today's business world.

Along with 'What is Customer Success?', C-Suite executives and many others are also asking 'Why would we invest in it?' 'Is the return going to be worth it?' 'What is this Customer Success "trend" all about anyway?!'

I enjoyed this post on LinkedIn which was shared while I was writing this chapter, by a member of the European, Middle East and Africa (EMEA) Customer Success community, Orkun Türkmen, in which he observes:

> Customer Success Management is like teenage sex: everyone at a Software-as-a-Service company talks about it, almost nobody really knows how to do it, everyone thinks everyone else is doing it, so everyone claims they are doing it...

As suggested in this post, Customer Success has its roots in the SaaS world, primarily B2B although all the principles are valid for B2C, and almost all businesses, come to that!

Venture Capitalists (VCs) are refusing to even consider investing in a SaaS start-up unless they can demonstrate they are invested in and sustaining a solid Customer Success department.

The reason for this is that there needs to be a department which is completely focused on driving and tracking predictable recurring revenue. Predictability is safe, stable and what the analysts are looking for.

Without Customer Success focused on retaining and growing customers, recurring revenue becomes an unpredictable black hole of churn, i.e. rapid loss of customers.

Without Customer Success, your Sales team needs to find new customers to replace the customers who do not feel compelled to stay with you. This means you will always be chasing your tail, rather than maximising the opportunity of retaining and growing your existing customers, at a fraction of the cost.

All companies, particularly those whose revenue model is based on subscriptions, should be very focused on customers, their outcomes and success as this is intrinsically tied to the company's own success.

Customer's Success = Company's Success

Their Success = Your Success

Customer Success = Customer Growth

Customer Growth = Revenue Growth

In a world where the customer is once again and more than ever, in control, every person working in B2C and especially B2B should also be thinking about what the customer wants.

This is what concerns those of us immersed in the world of Customer Success, it's what keeps us awake at night and full of joy when we see customers not only remaining with us but:

- Growing their use of our product
- Influencing the direction of our product and programme
- Advocating our services on our behalf
- Providing case studies and references
- Bringing new customers to our door

Your revenue growth engine

 Your existing customer portfolio base is your most efficient route to creating and maintaining a powerful revenue growth engine.

It is estimated that the cost of acquiring a new customer is between five and twenty-five times higher than it costs to retain an existing one.

It therefore makes sense to maximise the lifetime value of your existing customers. It is far cheaper and much more rewarding.

A 5% increase in your retention rates can increase profits by 25% to 95%

Bain & Company

These supremely important facts should be kept handy whenever you're asked to justify why Customer Success deserves any investment, let alone investment anywhere close to the scale of a Sales team. Customer Success, despite the shift in perception around customer focus, is still seen as the poor relation, with an ability to perform miracles on fumes alone. Fight your corner and get the investment you deserve to deliver that stratospheric growth at reduced costs relative to new sales.

To be clear, the task of maximising customer lifetime value is the job of everyone in an organisation. Without doubt, everyone has a part to play: Sales, Marketing, Product, Senior Management, Support, everyone!

There needs to be an aligned and cohesive approach with a transparent and validated belief in the organisation's commitment to customer focus and orientation.

See also 1.2 Foundations and Beliefs
3.3 Demonstrating Value

Customer Success can be visualised as a traditional process

Inputs > Process > Outputs

These are some of the inputs:

Figure 0.2: Customer Success Inputs

This is the 'processing' or activities for which the CS team are responsible:

Figure 0.3: Customer Success Processes

These are some of the outputs:

Figure 0.4: Customer Success Outputs

These are the inner workings of your growth engine and these are the expectations:

For the customer: they will have an expectation of what they will get from your service and how it will support their business goals, objectives and targets. It is imperative you discover, understand, capture and agree what these are and most importantly, how you will prove and measure this.

For the company: sustainable value generally boils down to customer retention and scalable growth through your customer portfolio which ensures a lower Customer Retention Cost (CRC) than Customer Acquisition Cost (CAC). This is achieved through organic growth made possible by your existing customer base expanding, the referrals from this base, and pollination due to champion users taking your service with them, when they move jobs to potential new customers and bringing you on board (aka second order revenue).

As a summary of where Customer Success stands as a function with its counterparts, see table below:

	Customer Success	Sales	Account management	Marketing	Support	Customer experience*
New business		Yes				
Lead generation				Yes		
Retention	Yes					
Up-sells	Yes		Yes			
Cross-sells	Yes		Yes			
Case studies	Yes			Yes		
Recurring revenue	Yes					
Proactive	Yes					
Reactive					Yes	
Operational					Yes	
Strategic	Yes					
First-line support					Yes	
Escalations and follow-up	Yes					
Coordinator	Yes					
Trusted advisor	Yes					
Sales target		Yes	Yes			
Compensation plan	Yes	Yes	Yes	Yes		
Measure experience						Yes
Optimise experience						Yes
Design for experience						Yes

* Customer Experience is essential to a customer-focused business. It is the imperative to consider each activity from the perspective of the customer.

Figure 0.5: Attributes of Customer Success and its counterparts

- All departments should be aware of and focused on Customer Success
- All departments should be commercially aware
  - ***Global: Every interaction is a potential income-generating (aka Sales) engagement***
- Customer Success should not have a Sales target to reach
  - Customer Success Managers (CSMs) should be trusted advisors and they cannot be deemed as such if they have an income number to achieve
- CSMs should absolutely have a compensation plan which includes other metrics, such as Net Retention Rate, Gross Retention Rate, Adoption, case studies, etc.
- Equally, other departments should have Customer Success components to their compensation plan
- Customer Success team should co-ordinate the alignment, consistency and focus of all business activities to ensure complete customer focus (see Figure 0.6)
- The achievement of good customer experience can be expressed as
  - Customer Experience = Customer Expectation
- Customer Success should exist to ensure a company-wide focus and alignment on the customer and their success
  - Their Success = Our Success

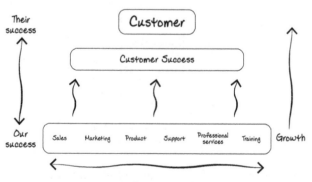

Figure 0.6: Alignment for Success

How to use this book

Customer Success is at a tipping point. CEOs and VCs, particularly in the B2B subscription world, know it should be a thing but no one knows what it really looks and feels like.

I want to share my experiences with my peers and colleagues and hear from others to understand the art of the possible.

We are pioneers; there is no set path yet and together we can shape the future. It's a really exciting and unusual time to be involved in such a nascent discipline.

You are a pioneer

Customer Success is an emerging discipline for professionals focused on customer outcomes, trust, loyalty, retention, referrals and growth.

As such, you are a pioneer, starting on this exciting journey.

This book will walk you through the first months of establishing a Customer Success function and philosophy which works in alignment with the rest of your organisation's teams to maximise your revenue growth engine, i.e. your customer portfolio.

The structure of this book

The book is divided into two parts:

- Part I is an introduction to Customer Success, the DIME framework and the book itself

- Part II contains the concepts involved in the DIME cycle and in building a successful Customer Success function

The DIME framework is deliberately cyclical and can be used in a micro and macro context. It can also be applied to the discipline of Customer Success and its evolution.

Each topic within this book has been, to a point, arbitrarily placed within a specific stage of the DIME cycle; this has been a matter of logistics. Each topic needs to sit somewhere although few of the topics are addressed sequentially, in practicality.

Within Customer Success, all the topics and themes are interconnected so there's lots of cross-pollination and organic growth; when you tend to one branch, another adapts and flourishes. They all need to be considered concurrently and many are interconnected.

For this reason, you will find cross-references included in the text in this format:

See also

The DIME concept works at a macro and a micro level and is based on a standard project approach to implementations:

- Research and design your scope
- Implement the proposed design
- Measure the impact of your delivery for success and alignment to desired objectives
- Use a phased approach to test each element before evolving and iterating

It does not matter with which topic you start; keep in mind the need to Design, Implement, Measure and Evolve each piece of work on which you focus (micro). It is also important to ensure that you address the overall programme and philosophy within your organisation (macro) to ensure that you are continually iterating and evolving using the DIME acronym.

This is also true of the Customer Success profession itself:

- Design: Salesforce becoming aware of a churn challenge
- Implement: Assign responsibility for addressing the churn issue
- Measure: Is this working? Are we retaining customers? Is this enough? Retaining customers is actually cheaper than acquiring new ones...
- Evolve: What can we do to maximise our retention and grow our revenue through our portfolio?
- Design: Rather than addressing a negative challenge, let's focus on the positive outcomes
- Implement: Work in partnership with customers to grow our recurring revenue organically
- And so on...

Therefore, please use this book in the manner which works for you. Pick the topic which is of highest priority or where you have the least knowledge and apply DIME on a micro level.

- Design your approach to applying this topic within your organisation
  - o Research the topic using this book and online resources
- Implement your chosen design
- Measure the impact and efficacy of this implementation
- Evolve your programme by iterating and adapting this topic or choose another area on which to focus

Prompts and appendices

This book contains a number of formatting prompts and appendices:

See also   where subjects are discussed in numerous areas of the book, this prompt will help you locate the additional information

this symbol is used when there is a key piece of information being shared

these are the end-of-chapter summaries which will list key learnings, actions and tips to remember

these items are optional reading and may contain anecdotal stories or additional reasoning for certain concepts

Glossary   there is a glossary included at the end of the book for terms and acronyms with which you may not be familiar

Resources   the resources section includes a non-exhaustive list of useful conferences, blogs, communities and meet-ups

Contact me

If you'd like to continue the conversation or have any further questions, please do not hesitate to contact me: talk@ thecspioneer.com

There will also be an evolving set of online resources at www. thecspioneer.com/resources

The four fundamental stages of the DIME cycle

A final word on the structure of this book and the four fundamental stages of the DIME cycle which we will use to demonstrate how to create, sustain, evolve and iterate a winning Customer Success function and philosophy within your business.

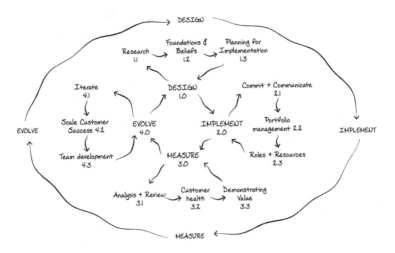

Figure 0.7: The DIME framework

It is important to note that this is a framework by which to order the content in the book. However, the order of the work which you wish to deliver may vary depending on the maturity of your business or the size and breadth of your portfolio, among many other factors.

See also Part I: How to use this book

There are four stages within the DIME cycle:

Design
- Research
  - Listen to your stakeholders, including your customers
    - Gather data and research ideas and options
- Foundations and beliefs
  - Understand the support and challenges in relation to commitment to Customer Success and any existing programme
- *Plan* your programme and data capture
  - Design your process, programme, roles and responsibilities and outcomes, involving your key stakeholders
  - Explicitly *agree* the outputs from the design phase with all your key stakeholders, particularly your customers
- Collaborate at every phase of the cycle, ensuring roles and responsibilities are understood, delivered and adapted as necessary

Implement
- *Commit to and communicate* your programme to all key stakeholders, ensuring agreement and buy-in is sustained
- Adopt *portfolio management* to achieve your objectives proactively and effectively
- Understand your Roles and Resources
  - Ensure virtual resources are exploited and commitment is granted
- Transition from reactive to proactive

Measure
- Undertake regular *Analysis and Review* to ensure your objectives are on track
  - o Measure the impact of your proactive programming
  - o Benchmark your achievements, results and programme
- Establish an accurate and usable *Customer Health* system
- *Demonstrate the value* of Customer Success to your team, company, customers and other stakeholders

Evolve
- *Iterate* to the next evolution, based on the output of the Measure stage
  - o What works? What could be improved?
  - o *Adapt* the programme, processes, roles and responsibilities and outcomes
    - ▪ Based on the data gathered
- *Scale* your programme and processes
  - o In alignment with your strategic plan
  - o Based on experience to date, customer sentiment and industry trends
- Build and develop your *team*
  - o Team mate success
  - o Human connections and relationships
  - o Skills and compensation

Defined in its essence as a cycle, there is room and necessity to iterate over time, as with any enduring, successful and adaptive framework. Therefore, any changes identified during the Evolve stage of the DIME cycle should then be iterated through the four stages.

Pioneer's round–up!

Key learnings

❖ Customer Success is being fully and demonstrably committed to knowing and understanding your customer. The business of having this focus is a life or death issue for your organisation

❖ Customer Success is the result of LTV being realised over many contract periods rather than upfront
  ❑ Recurring Income vs Capital Expenditure

❖ Your existing customer portfolio base is your most efficient route to creating and maintaining a powerful revenue growth engine

❖ It is estimated that the cost of acquiring a new customer (CAC) is between five and twenty-five times higher than it costs to retain an existing one (CRC)

❖ Customer Success is the responsibility of all. The team of Customer Success is one of co-ordination and communication

Actions

❖ Undertake your own research into what Customer Success means to you and your company; use the Resources content at the back of this book to get you started. Find and talk to your peers; make connections

❖ Review your Inputs–Processing–Outputs (Figures 0.2–0.4) to prepare for the Design stage of the DIME cycle

❖ Understand which teams and functions exist in your business: are they aligned and collaborative or are they working in silos? Consider their objectives, targets and goals: are they geared towards a common focus?

❖ Familiarise yourself with the DIME framework
❖ Identify which topic is most relevant to you now and start there and apply the micro DIME approach
  ❏ NB: It's also ok to work through the book in sequence!

Hot tips
❖ Their Success = Your Success
❖ Customer Growth = Revenue Growth

＊

For more ideas and templates, download the companion workbook at www.thecspioneer.com/resources/workbook

Get in touch to share your thoughts, questions, challenges and triumphs: talk@thecspioneer.com

II

DESIGN. IMPLEMENT. MEASURE. EVOLVE (DIME)

1.0 DIME cycle stage: Design

The groundwork required to design your revenue growth

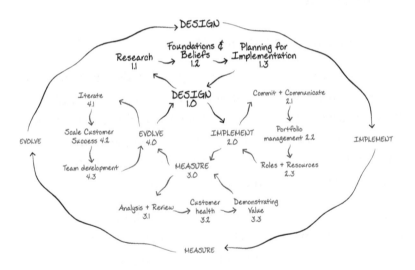

There are a few key topics within the DESIGN stage of the cycle

- *Taking stock:* researching and listening to the data, facts and opinions of others
- *Foundations and beliefs:* strong foundations are imperative for a successful journey and it's an area to be reviewed and aligned as soon as possible
- *Use data to plan your approach:* strong decisions and designs need to be based on data, it is therefore of vital importance to understand to which data you have access and whether there is more that needs to be identified

1.1 Research

1.1.1 Listening and taking stock

The first stage of the DIME cycle is DESIGN and before we can even begin to think about what the future should look like, we need to take stock to understand what has happened thus far. This might be within your own company, within your customers, the evolution of Customer Success trends, your previous experience and that of your peers.

We need to understand where we are and how we got here to create an effective approach for the future. We need to learn from our experiences and build out from the status quo.

Therefore, the very first action within the DIME cycle is to Listen. Listen to your customers, listen to your C-Suite, listen to your fellow colleagues, listen to the data.

It is important to be prepared so that you understand:

- The explicit value-add of your Customer Success offering
- Your connection to your customers
- Your capabilities, processes and messaging
- The internal alignment, responsibilities, activities and communication
- Your role
- How to articulate to the customer how you will help them
- The impact of your function for your customers, your internal teams and the revenue line

Customer portfolio

Some of the questions you will probably already be asking yourself are:

- Who are our customers?
- Why did they buy the products/services they have?
  - This will be an important input into understanding their objectives and what they think success will look like
- Where are they in their journey and lifecycle with us?
- When is their contract up for renewal?
- Have we engaged with them yet and if so, how, when, how often and when was the last time?
- What does their usage and adoption look like?
- Are they likely to renew?
- Which contracts are at risk?

Understanding your portfolio is critical at whichever stage of maturity your business has achieved. In the early days, every customer is significant and every detail can win or lose you the renewal. As the portfolio grows, it will be important to segment and prioritise the level of service and type of engagement utilised

Review the existing files and records and ensure they are complete to your satisfaction.

Use this data to prioritise your immediate activities; we know that you'll still need to manage your existing portfolio while doing your listening and researching. Assign a RAG (Red, Amber, Green) status for the time being and get to work on those with the highest priority.

The status may be based on:

- Closest renewal date
- Largest contract value
- Low utilisation/adoption rates
- Customer experience to date
  - e.g. Knowledge of an unstable relationship which needs fixing.

Your framework and portfolio management will improve and become more sophisticated as you progress through your DIME process.

See also 2.2 Portfolio management
3.2 Customer Health

Why did they buy?
The reason for buying will play a significant role in your partnership with the customer. Ultimately, we are looking for a successful partnership with our customers. Expectations, responsibilities and commitments from each party should have been framed at the outset and reviewed on a periodic basis.

If this has not been done, take the opportunity as you engage with each customer to do it now.

A common debate you will or may already have heard is that Customer Success is not about making customers happy. It is about making them successful. You will also hear that many Customer Success professionals prefer to hear from their 'unhappy' customers, as their feedback forces them to continually challenge and develop the status quo.

My assertion would be that successful *and* happy should be possible. A customer can be happy *because* your partnership is a successful one.

 The key to success is understanding your customers' reason for buying and using your service:

- What are their expectations?
- What are the outcomes for which they are striving?
- How are you able to contribute to those outcomes?
- How will it be measured?

This information will, hopefully, have been captured during the sales cycle which took place before the contract was signed (pre-sales). If this has never previously been done, it's a great opportunity to engage with your customer.

Talk to your customer to identify what their desired outcomes are and how these align to your services and products. Make commitments *which you can keep* and ensure the customer invests in the partnership by accepting relevant actions they need to progress to get to their outcomes.

Understanding their needs and expectations and being able to demonstrate measurable progress towards them will make a considerable difference in their view of you as a trusted advisor and valuable partner. This trust will lead to loyalty, retention, growth, advocacy and referrals.

Past relationship history

It is important to get to grips with the relationship history from anyone who has already had interactions with the customer. This information is also important to build up as part of your standard delivery programme, once you've designed it.

See also 1.3 Planning for Implementation

- How long have they been a customer?
- How many contact points do you have in their company?
  - How broad and deep is the relationship? This can be particularly important if a main sponsor moves to another role or company
- How many are advocates and coaches for your service/product?
- Do you have access to and sponsorship from senior management and finance?
  - The people who sign the cheque/contract!
- Does the relationship work as a trusted partnership?
- How was the onboarding process?
  - How was the handover from sales > onboarding > CSM?
  - How long until time-to-value?

- o Were they trained successfully?
- What does their support history look like?
  - o Too much or too little interaction could indicate challenges

Stakeholders

With every customer and within your own company, you will be dealing with individuals. Research shows that whilst we work on behalf of our company, we buy from the people with whom we connect and trust.

As a Customer Success professional, it is imperative to create a trusted partnership with your customers. To achieve the status of Trusted Advisor as a Customer Success professional is vital.

Each of us, and this includes your customers, likes to do business with and stay loyal to the people we trust.

Taking stock of your position should, therefore, include understanding the connections you have in each of your customers' organisations as well as your own.

- C-Suite
- Internal function heads and team
  - o Sales
    - There is a history of friction between Customer Success and Sales teams so it's important to get them onside immediately
    - They are generally a sociable bunch so mix with them, get to know their personalities and what drives their loyalties and motivations
    - They are good at relationships, getting to people, and customer stakeholder mapping (see below) is

vital in ensuring an account stays alive, grows and becomes a referral

- Marketing
  - At some point, if you're not already, you'll want to send communications to your customer. Get expert help and accountability from the team who know what they are doing
  - Events, whether they are small and informal or large like a customer conference, take a lot of planning, time and effort. Enlist the right people from the start!
- Support
  - Frontline support are heroes, they remove all the repetitive, easily-solved approaches from the customer. Ensure you align and work with them in the right way. Keep them involved in your plans and communicate any changes so they remain on-message at all the key customer touchpoints
- Training
- Product
  - Customer Success is a hard place to be, if you don't have a solid product and a transparent relationship with those who decide its future and maintenance. Understand who you need to work with and develop a close and sharing relationship fast
  - You will also identify through this process that Product is who you need to work with to get the right customer usage data, and allow effective reporting to the customer
  - Ultimately, you must work with Product to ensure your software fulfils your customer needs, with an

imperative and user experience that compels them to use it consistently. This 'stickiness' will be your secret sauce and support you on your journey to adoption, loyalty and growth

- o Professional Services
- Economic Buyers (people who sign the contract, within your customer's company)
- End users of your product
- Champions of your product
- Influencers within your customers' organisations

It is a core part of the Sales cycle to understand who your stakeholders are and the relationship between them and you. This is equally important in the world of Customer Success. We need to understand the relationships, the power and the politics of the customers with whom we work.

This is called a stakeholder map and should be started by the Account Manager/Sales Director responsible for any customer. This should then, ideally, be held in the customer folder and updated whenever there is a change in personnel at the customer's company.

As part of your discovery journey, identify stakeholder maps which:

- Exist and are up to date
- Exist but need updating
- Do not exist

For the latter two categories, I would work with the Sales Account Manager responsible and ensure that there is one for each customer by the time you have finished your 'taking stock' activity.

Customer Success is about making and maintaining valuable connections

Customer Success can only work if there is a team of stakeholders working towards a united and agreed goal.

Framework and processes

Finally, you will need to understand how your organisation has been implementing Customer Success, if at all, to date.

- Are there any frameworks, models and processes in place?
- Have expectations been set with the customer?
  - Have these been met or missed?
- Has the customer lifecycle and journey been mapped?
- Is there a Customer Success programme definition?
- Are there a defined mission, vision and objectives for the Customer Success function?

What processes and framework exist?

At my organisation, without a formal Customer Success approach, we had been pretty ad-hoc and customer-led. In the early days, with only one or two leading-edge customers, this had been possible to facilitate. However, this can lead to headaches at this stage and into the future:

- The customer gets used to privileged treatment
  - This cannot be sustained so a transition plan needs to be created and communicated while maintaining a healthy and trustful relationship

- Internally, there is a mindset that we give each customer premium and high-touch care
  - This is also unsustainable and a set of processes and parameters need to be defined, communicated and understood by everyone

- The challenges increase for every customer brought on board before the clearly defined framework has been put in place

Each of these challenges is intrinsically linked to the others and are resolvable if you give immediate attention to understanding what you want your approach to be and communicate that to everyone whose work touches the customer. That's everyone at your company, by the way! And don't forget to welcome the customers to the new world too. They'll be pleased to have a clear path to walk.

Remember to work with each team at your company to understand the customer journey: how does the customer join us, when do they get passed from team to team and who is currently responsible for what?

For us, we had a Sales Account Manager who led the Sales cycle and they worked with a pre-sales team. Together, they gathered all that precious data we were discussing earlier (business problems, why did they buy, stakeholder maps, etc.) and handed it over to the Implementation team and ultimately the Support team, once they had gone live on the system.

At that point, records were not entirely updated, some customers got usage reporting, some did not, some got refresher training, some did not. This was not planned or proactive. It depended who asked us for something, and if we could provide it we would.

As a result of the process and framework investigation, I discovered and made note of the following:

- Current customer journey mapping (MS Word)
- Flag in the customer 'Bible' for Reporting Yes/No (Excel)
- Existing documentation gathered together and made accessible to all in a customer folder (Sharepoint)
  - Customer pilot documents
  - Customer sales cycle documents
  - Stakeholder map
  - Customer reporting
  - Customer journey map and current roles/responsibilities

Pioneer's round-up!

Key learnings

❖ Listen to your Customers, C-Suite, Peers and data

❖ Customer Success is about making and maintaining valuable connections
  - ❑ Customers => Trusted Advisor
  - ❑ Stakeholders => Collaborations, Communication and Alignment

❖ Understanding the content, status and priorities of your customer portfolio is at the heart of Customer Success activities
  - ❑ Keep simple, to begin with and evolve with each iteration of your development

❖ It is key to know and understand the connections between your service/product and customer outcomes and expectations
  - ❑ Drive your customers towards successful attainment of their goals
  - ❑ Embed your service into their processes to ensure a long-term partnership

Actions

❖ Review your customer Portfolio
  - ❑ Ensure it is complete with all required details
  - ❑ Assign a status and priority

❖ Ensure a stakeholder map exists
  - ❑ For each of your customers (work in collaboration with your Sales team)

- ❑ For your team and your future vision, making sure you include
  - Existing network
  - Customers
  - Internal stakeholders
  - Team mates and community
- ❖ Identify and document the existing framework and processes which are already in place
  - ❑ Audit existing customer journey

See also 1.3.2 Define your programme for outcomes and success

Hot tips
- ❖ The reasons why your customers buy your product is intrinsically linked to their required business outcomes
  - ❑ Their Outcomes = Their Success = Your Success
- ❖ Ensure your product is 'sticky'

***

For more ideas and templates, download the companion workbook at www.thecspioneer.com/resources/ workbook

Get in touch to share your thoughts, questions, challenges and triumphs: talk@thecspioneer.com

1.2 Success is made of strong foundations and firm beliefs

It is imperative that the entire organisation takes responsibility and understands the part they play in achieving their customer's outcomes and therefore, success so that they, in turn, maximise their own company's success, their team's success and finally their own success.

Their Success = Your Success

Understanding the true values of your organisation, including your mission and vision for the Customer Success function, is imperative and will provide you with the strong foundations to plan your journey towards the destination of sustainable customer growth and success.

Foundations

The foundation for any successful team effort is to understand the make-up of each contributing part and using the strengths of each to formulate the best approach for the task at hand.

Initial steps for gathering information related to your foundations and beliefs are:

- Consider your own thoughts, principles, research and objectives first
- Gather information and opinions from your C-Suite to understand
  - Where they fit in the organisation
  - How they are aligned to Customer Success
  - Who is truly enshrined in the philosophy of putting the customer and relationships first

- If and how much 'selling' you need to do with each of them and their team
- With any new process, it is always key to involve every level of the organisation. If you involve people in the creation of the process, they are more likely to accept and adopt it
  - Managers are therefore important to understand, rather than purely acting on the opinions and expectations of their C-level reporting line
  - In the same vein, the guys at the frontline, who are doing all the daily work, supporting the customers at the moment and probably getting all the flack; they are the guys from whom you really want to make sure you get no holds barred feedback
- Customers
  - Do your customers currently feel that they are put first, and is this in alignment with the findings from your internal research?
  - Always talk to your customers and avoid assumptions and confusion

Define, agree and cultivate your Customer Success vision

First step, then, is to formulate your mission and vision. This is important for these reasons:

- A clear vision and mission statement will give you a firm basis for the approach and structures you will choose to put in place, to achieve your objectives
- From your position of clarity, you will be able to articulate your elevator pitch efficiently and effectively
  - The C-Suite needs to be bought in and working for you and your customers, so you must get your point across

succinctly and powerfully. Their attention span is limited as they have a thousand and one calls on their time!

o Every team and individual are critical to the mission of Customer Success and you need to be able to express, in a way that is impactful, their role in it

o Oftentimes, customers are perplexed by the differing contact points and teams with whom they interact. Being able to clearly articulate the value and outcomes which you will help drive will create a solid and connected partnership

• The vision and mission will give you, and everyone involved, a defined focus from which to start, get aligned and a benchmark against which to check every movement, development and objective

As identified above, it is important that the vision and mission incorporate internal and external communications and stakeholders.

Get your own thoughts in order

Whether a topic is new to you or you feel like a seasoned veteran, there's always something new to learn. Additionally, Customer Success is an emerging and therefore rapidly evolving discipline. Ideas are forming and transforming on a regular basis and it's good to keep up, formulate your own position on the topic and if you feel like it, add your voice to the discussion. It's an exciting time to be involved as you can be part of the revolution, helping to shape the future of Customer Success and the wider world of the customer!

In your first year within Customer Success, research will be powerful for additional reasons; it will help you form your perspective of what you want your offering to achieve and this, in turn, will support your effectiveness at articulating and communicating this to your key stakeholders – C-Suite, Management, Internal teams, your team and your customers.

There are many sources and channels of research and in my first year, I scoured my area for all and any that I could find and interrogate.

Availability, accessibility and structure of many of these channels have vastly improved since my first year in Customer Success, and the whole profession is searching for each other and pulling together.

For further assistance, review:

- The Glossary and Resources sections of this book
- www.thecspioneer.com/resources

Beliefs

How many of us work in a company which claims to be 'customer-centric'?

How many of us truly work in a company which IS customer-centric?

How can you tell whether the company which claims to be customer-focused, really is?

There are a few key indicators to look out for and review when understanding your company's position on Customer Success and ensuring that a philosophy permeates the whole organisation:

- CEO

  It is of utmost importance that the CEO not only talks the talk but walks the walk. They must be concerned with the power of human connections and relationships – within the company, between teams and with every customer – and prove, through action and guiding values, that this is the case ensuring the entire company follows suit

- C-Suite

  A top-down philosophy is a must and therefore the CEO needs to be surrounded with like-minded colleagues. The C-Suite needs to understand the power of the customer and of being customer-focused

  It will also be illuminating to understand how Customer Success is represented within the C-Suite; for example, is there a Chief Customer Officer?

- Reporting Line

  There are many arguments for where Customer Success should sit in an organisation and this will change as an organisation matures in its thinking about the philosophy and the function itself (regardless of the size and maturity of the organisation itself).

  Understand where the team sits and how much voice it has at the top table, to understand how important the philosophy is to the company.

See also 4.3 Team development

- Product

  Is the product customer-focused and is the roadmap driven by customer-centric features and functionality? Are there any Customer Advisory Boards (CAB) or user groups where feedback is welcomed, gathered and utilised in considering the future for the product?

You will have gathered a fair amount of data relating to the existing beliefs of the organisation through the activity you undertook in your research activities.

Get to know your C-Suite and who's in your corner

If you're going to have a customer-focused philosophy, the C-Suite, led by the CEO, must understand the true nature of Customer Success and the need for a company-wide, top-down culture.

It will help you to understand the truth within your organisation; you will need entirely different approaches depending on whether you truly believe you have a customer philosophy at your company or if you have to start your personal journey by spreading the gospel according to the Customer Success pioneers.

With an ingrained philosophy, you will find it much easier to gain approval from the C-Suite to design and implement a function which will achieve your mission and vision. You will know that each of your executives are motivating their teams to work *with* you and your team to achieve that mission and vision. You will have the commitment of each and every member of the organisation to do their bit to achieve the company's mission to maximise sustainable growth through the customer growth engine.

I believe that this is the root cause for the failure of the majority of Customer Success functions. Without the dedicated commitment of the senior management team, you can sweat blood and tears, be a passionate advocate for your customers and your programming, be a martyr to the cause and yet, the team will still fold.

The foundation has to be strong and it has to be built on the firm belief from the C-Suite understanding the importance of the existing customer base to become the most powerful growth engine.

> *We all know that some executives talk the talk*
> *but do they walk the walk?*

This question is why this topic should be part of your research phase. During the interview stage or through whichever route you've landed where you are now, the right people may have said the right things. They may even have been backed up by their teams. How can you be sure though? One thing I have learned is that actions speak louder than words. The philosophy should be embodied by every single person within the organisation and this needs to start at the top.

The first question when a new idea or concept is raised should be – how will this impact the customer? How will it help the customer?

If the customer question is brought to the table late in the discussion, not at all or by only one person, this is a warning sign that more work needs to be done on your company's values and focus.

 At Artesian, it started at the top. While the trigger for building a dedicated Customer Success function was eventually motivated by external factors (VC talks and the knowledge that it would become an imperative in the near future and we wanted to be ahead of the curve), we were already a customer-focused organisation. Our early funding came from a Professional Services arm of the business, so we'd always known the importance of client relationships, repeat business, customer retention, growth and referrals for new business.

Our Chief Executive Officer (CEO), Andrew Yates, embodied customer focus. How do I know? Because actions speak louder than words.

At the inception of Customer Success, I reported into the Chief Operating Officer (COO) and yet Andrew was constantly asking what was in it for the customer. Every programme, activity and meeting we put in place had to have a positive impact on and for the customer. He understood that value for them was inherently value for us.

I once heard a speaker at a conference say that a good indicator is to observe how much time the CEO spent visiting customers versus time locked away in their office. I could honestly say that Andrew spent most of his time with customers and encouraged as much of the company as possible to hear what our customers had to say at every opportunity.

We brought customers into our offices to gather input for our internal projects and ran a Product Enhancement Programme (PEP), which was an advisory board featuring a range of customers so we could get a good, customer-focused steer on the product roadmap.

He invested in Customer Success, much earlier than many start-up SaaS businesses because he knew it made sense. He didn't need to be convinced of its importance. Of course, as we grew, we needed to demonstrate value and build a business case for further investment as resources are always finite! (*See also* 3.3 Demonstrating Value) This meant that, with a smaller starting portfolio, I was able to implement a well-defined structure rather than being in constant firefighting mode. Proactive rather than reactive.

More than that, though, he gave his time to the Customer Success team and, most importantly, to our customers. The big and the small. The happy and the unhappy. The successful and unsuccessful. All with an aim to understand how our service added value, how we could add more value and how we could help the customer achieve their outcomes.

Key indicators to identify their level of commitment
Unearth the company documents

- Company policies
- Company mission
- Core values
- Customer policy
- Governance
- Compensation plans and policies

Do the contents of these documents translate into customer focus? Would and do they motivate everyone in the company to focus on the customer and their outcomes? Do the compensation plans promote customer focus?

If there are no written policies, go back to the same key stakeholders and see what they say (if you've peeked ahead, you'll know that you should also watch *how* they say it).

- C-Suite; make sure you talk to each of them
- Managers
- Frontline
- Customers

Observe
If the company documents say it is customer-focused does this stay true in the day-to-day activities of the organisation? Or are they just words which have been written/spoken to you, because 'everyone is doing/saying it, so we should do the same'?

Talk to and observe the key players
A deeper level of observation and discussion should be undertaken with the key officers within your organisation. Get to the heart of what drives them, how you can help them and how they in turn will help you.

Here are some of the observations, questions and considerations I have made in my experiences over the years:

- Chief Executive Officer (CEO)
  - As with Andrew at Artesian, observe whether the commander-in-chief is ever with customers or are

they too busy or too important to deal with individual customers?

○ Which words do they use? Do they ever change? Are they repeating a script or waxing lyrical about a subject for which they have real drive and passion?

○ Do they motivate their teams, identifying with them and creating relationships? If they care about their internal customers (i.e. their staff), they are more likely to believe in the customer-focused philosophy. After all, this philosophy is about putting people first and in the end that comes down to all people

- Chief Technology Officer (CTO)/Chief Information Officer (CIO)
  ○ Product alignment to the customer is key so it is worth investigating how often the Product team interact with your customers and through which channels
- Chief Operating Officer (COO)
  ○ Oftentimes, Professional Services, Support, Training and Enablement are key relationship teams within an organisation
  ○ These are going to be or already are some of your key partners. They are committed to supporting the customer so are most likely to be your easiest and closest allies
- Chief Finance Officer (CFO)
  ○ This person holds the key to investment in Customer Success and customer focus
  ○ If you aren't already on the best of terms, find a way to their heart! Ensure they understand the impact of sustainable revenue growth through your philosophy

and programming and you'll be able to encourage the investment you need

- Chief Revenue Officer (CRO)/Chief Sales Officer (CSO)
  - Historically, there has been friction between Sales and Customer Success as some Sales teams feel there's a battle for commission on sales and new opportunities within existing customers
  - As with all other departments, there should be a strong partnership between these particular teams. They both want the same thing and with the customer at the heart of things, revenue growth will be easier
- CxO
  - Do you have other officers in your C-Suite?
  - Who are they?
  - What is their mission?
  - For example, Chief Customer Officer (CCO)

Is there a CCO? This is not the standard operating framework yet, although there are some exceptional examples of CCOs leading the customer revolution within companies. The drive is to get a seat at the C-level table, to ensure that the customer perspective is being presented without any distracting bias.

If you're in a leading-edge company, which has already appointed a CCO, what are their responsibilities? This will also help you understand if customer focus is an ingrained value or if the C-Suite are paying lip service for the benefit of their investors or due to peer pressure and current 'trends'.

I put 'trend' in quotation marks /air-marks/rabbit-ears, for a reason.

Some company officers and other employees will see Customer Success as just that. A trend, something to be tolerated, a buzz-term to use for a while and then return to normal, once the dust has settled. This is a symptom of the field being so embryonic, a seedling if you will, in a forest of professions and business concepts.

See also 3.3 Demonstrating Value

Outcomes

- What are the stated business goals, mission and vision and the business outcomes expected in order to achieve this strategic aim?
    - a. Does this embody the philosophy of being customer-focused
- Are the C-Suite saying the right words and following these up by ensuring they are always taking actions which are aligned to your customer-focused policies and values? If they are doing this, they are leading by example and you're onto a winning situation. Company core values come from the actions of the CEO primarily and flow down the hierarchy. If you have a strong behaviour at the top, you tend to find that the company follows.
- Are the business outcomes aligned to the customer outcomes which you've established through your period of taking stock, researching and understanding your mission and vision for Customer Success?

What do you need from them?
During this period of research and analysis, you will come to understand what you need from each of the business areas and

key officers, both strategically and tactically. You will also be able to assess if there is a gap between what they believe are their responsibilities and/or what they and their teams already do to support them.

Crucially, you can also identify the value that you bring and how you can add your support to their mission to make their lives easier.

See also 3.3 Demonstrating Value

We talked earlier about creating stakeholder maps; these are of vital importance for your customers, during the sales process and evolving throughout the customer lifecycle. They are also really useful for your own processes and programmes, to understand who are your champions (internally and externally), who you can count on when you're driving investment and improvements to your business process and also those with whom you need to create a closer alliance (e.g. Sales and Product teams are two to focus on here; a mutually respectful and supportive partnership with each of these teams is key to our movement).

 The stakeholder map will also uncover the power of influence within your organisation and this will help you navigate your way through discussions and negotiations with ease.

With all the information you have gathered through the research stages, you will also be creating new alliances where there are currently silos or perhaps even conflicts, and solidifying those partnerships which are inevitably already stronger due to obvious parallels in missions.

Current Sales process

As part of your observations, watch the current process from pre-sale through signature and then into post-sale.

How is the customer 'sold-to'? Is there discussion over the desired outcomes and how they will be achieved, together, with the product capability?

What happens as the ink is drying or after it has dried?

Implementation? Support? Renewals?

How is the customer treated? If there is an existing role or department covering Customer Success, are they included at any point? If so, which?

A controversial point to put into print but which needs to be raised: we all know that with some Sales teams, particularly at key moments in the financial year (quarter-end, half-year and year-end!), there is a tendency to do *anything* to get a customer across the line – any customer, whether they are a good fit or not. All of this just to meet a personal quota, or because the Sales team is revenue-focused rather than customer-focused.

The wrong customer can be very costly.

- A wrong customer is a customer who has shown interest in your product and, after due diligence, it would have been proven they do not match your target market or ideal customer. These companies exist and it's ok to say no and even refer them to an alternative solution
  - you shouldn't see this as sending them to a competitor as you wouldn't make this customer successful;
  - in this way, you get a good reputation for doing the right thing
- If they have been brought on, in a hurry, with less than due diligence performed and as a result of attaining some time-bound quota, then the chances are they will have very favourable contract terms
- Due to the wrong fit, you will inevitably spend much more effort in onboarding, supporting and managing this customer
- You may persuade them to renew once or even a few times, depending on the length of the contract
- Ultimately, though, they will leave
  - If they've had a bad experience despite all your best efforts, they could become a detractor and spread negative reviews amongst your ideal target customers
  - Even if they appreciate all the extra work you put in, if you were to analyse the cost vs income of that particular customer, you will find they have cost you significantly more to nurse through the process without longer term or growth benefits

At the management level, a strong decision needs to be made about ensuring the company understands for whom the product will achieve the desired results and about having the courage to walk away from customers who don't match this analysis. This is difficult for any company at any size and maturity and much harder for those in a start-up environment. It is, however, the right decision. Stay focused; on your vision and on your target customers.

At the frontline, it is well known that the majority of Sales teams are made up of strong, A-type individuals who are heavily motivated by their compensation plan. It is, therefore, crucial that the compensation plan of a customer-focused business reflects that business imperative.

See also 4.3 Team development

As a demonstration of walking the walk, there is definitely a case for the voice of the customer to be present during the sales cycle. This is one of the major reasons you must closely align to your CRO to ensure that the Customer Success team is involved, or at the very least informed, during the sales cycle. Conversely, the Sales team would always be involved and at the very least informed during all 'post-sales' activities.

It is evident, as the Subscription and Outcomes eras rise to prominence, that there is no longer such a thing as pre- and post-sales. We are all, always, in a Sales position with our prospects and customers, as we want them to renew, expand and refer us to their peers and network.

Role and reporting line

This is a much debated topic within Customer Success and businesses, as a whole, which embrace the customer-focused approach.

There is no definitive or 'right' answer. It will depend on any number of factors, some of the most prevalent of which are listed here:

- Size of company
- Number and value of customer portfolio
- Maturity of company
  - Processes
  - Product
  - People
  - Philosophy
- The existence of a CCO
- The extent to which customer-centricity is embedded in the company
- Maturity of customer portfolio
  - Length of contracts
  - Stability of customer renewals/loyalty

See also 1.3 Planning for Implementation
4.3 Team development

Role of Customer Success
Here are a few areas that you might want to consider how the customer fits now to understand current dynamics, and which will also be a base from which to build for the future.

As a general rule, how do other teams and departments work with Customer Success? Is there a partnership and language such as 'our account' and 'our customer' or are the Customer Success Managers (CSMs) kept away from the account and tasked with activities?

With a true customer philosophy embodied in every person and every activity, you will hear inclusive language and see teams naturally working together; team silos and pockets of information should be a thing of the past. Once everyone understands the equation that THEIR SUCCESS = MY SUCCESS this will be the standard way of doing business. It is up to management to create a culture, an environment and a structure which encourages rather than inhibits this.

At a number of companies I know, part of employee onboarding includes shadowing each team so that everyone understands each other's role and how everything fits together. I would encourage you to do the same and ask members of other teams to shadow your team too. What is it they say, 'walk a mile in someone's shoes' to truly understand their experiences.

As part of this specific process, I propose a similar activity. Look at the current processes to see who gets involved, with whom, at which point and for what purpose. Does it make sense, does it promote a sense of 'one team' and does it promote customer first?

A few examples are described here:

Pre-signature: what happens during the sales process?
Which teams are involved? Is there a pre-sales team? Does Customer Success get involved? Should they?

A key topic to cover is whether your voice is heard and taken seriously. For example, if a sale is clearly not fit for purpose – the customer will not get the benefits they are expecting – does anyone put up their hand and say 'We should walk away from this sale. We are not going to deliver for this customer, they will not get value and therefore, neither will we'. And if they do (or you did for the first time), would that make a difference?

Customer selection is important in the Sales process and in the enthusiasm to get every account across the line, this is often forgotten about in the Sales environment. They pass it over to post-sales and it's now 'their problem' in the head of the sales person.

There are companies who do take this seriously. Not only does the customer lead get a seat at the table for these deal reviews, but they have full veto power.

Onboarding
There's a lot of literature out there detailing how the first 100, or even thirty days are crucial to keeping a customer for life. How does this work at your company? Who gets involved? Does Customer Success? Should it?

Escalation
Who does this go to, how does it flow, who is ultimately responsible, who talks to the customer?

Customer marketing
This is a complex area. Does it and should it sit with Marketing or Customer Success?

I'm not saying that Customer Success should have full responsibility for every process in the organisation (although, there is at least one organisation who has given this reporting structure a lot of time and attention) but there should be awareness, involvement and communication across all teams and processes which involve the customer. In a customer-focused company, that is *everything*.

- All the above
- Training
- First-Line Support
- Technical Support
- Revenue closing
  - Renewal
  - Upsell
  - Cross-sell

Reporting line for Customer Success

The reporting structure can also tell you a lot about the foundations of the company and whether it is truly customer-centric.

There's at least one organisation, in Europe, which has been through a couple of iterations with their reporting structure and got to a point where their CCO was the main Revenue officer. That's right, Sales reported into the CCO to ensure that every person was totally customer-focused to maximise that efficient growth engine!

This is, at the moment, a rare situation. However it certainly shows you that this company meant business, they were incredibly serious about putting the customer at the heart of everything they do.

You will, no doubt, find that the reporting line and possibly the responsibilities of the function will evolve and change over time. Relax and be comfortable with that knowledge. It will happen. It has happened and continues to happen to us all. It's ok.

There is no silver bullet here and no right or wrong answer; different organisations make different structures and cultures work for them. Review the options, along with the data you've gathered about your own company and make a decision, which you think will work for you as a starting point.

The key takeaway is to make the decision to change the roles and responsibilities whenever it's apparent this would best serve the customer and your company. The follow-up is to ensure that you define the new roles and responsibilities and communicate to everyone, including your customers. Through clarity, you avoid confusion!

See also 4.3 Team development

Other key partnerships and stakeholders

You've heard the saying 'It takes a village to raise a child'?

This saying has been adapted to fit pretty much every situation and now it is often used in its abbreviated form ('it takes a village') to prove a point that you need a team around you. No one is or should be expected to undertake a mighty task alone. We all need a network of support, and everyone around you wants to be part of that network and wants you to succeed.

Equally, if you proactively involve people, they are more likely to embrace your ideas and adopt the approach for going forward.

> Tell me and I will forget, show me and I may remember; involve me and I will understand.
>
> *Confucius*

If you've ever been in Sales or worked with Sales teams, you may know that they will work up a stakeholder map and also a Map of Influence. This is all to do with account planning. The same applies for Customer Success, whether you're looking at how to manage your customers or looking at your company. These techniques are all designed to get us where we want, to whom we want and what we want!

Time is limited, use it wisely. Understand the players in your environment and how you can help each other, whether they are your customers or colleagues.

Other key partnerships and stakeholders you may want to bring into your village:

- Everyone in your organisation
  I appreciate that sounds like *a lot* of people and it might be if you work for a large organisation.
    o Make sure you understand what each team contributes to the company's mission and then what you need from them for the Customer Success mission
    o Engage with them and get them to support your process and activities
- CSM Community
    o There are communities out there, join them and ask them for help. Contribute from your own experiences
    o Attend the conferences which are being delivered by the CSM technology vendors and communities
    o Attend related conferences; Customer Success is beginning to surface more regularly in many others like SaaStock and SaaStr
    o Engage with a mentor/mentee programme or find your own relationship(s)

- These are becoming more prevalent, particularly in EMEA
- Become a mentor for someone as well as finding your valuable mentor

NB: There is a list of resources later in the book to help with your quest here. Equally, all the information, templates and a workbook will be on the website: www.thecspioneer.com

- Customers
Much as using everyone in your company will help lighten the load, so will using your customers. We have already mentioned and will talk in more depth about the relationship between you and your customer. Remember: Their Success = Your Success and vice versa.
  - There are a number of key roles within a customer that you will want to identify, some are easier than others
    - Sponsors
    - Champions
    - Coaches
  - You will also be looking to your customers to provide you with referrals; this is a significant part of the organic and accelerated customer growth engine process, whether the referrals are formally through your marketing processes or informally through peer-to-peer conversations about you!
  - Bring your own application (BYOA)

    This phenomenon began with the advent of free software flooding the market in an attempt to get a large non-paying customer base which would then be transitioned to an irresistible 'premium' offering, for which you would have to pay. LinkedIn is a prime example of this. It began as a single user, personal use account and has evolved over the years to a company-paid business premium offering. In the early days of this trend, people would take their favoured apps with them from company to company. This is becoming less applicable as IT clamps down on security and as companies choose preferred solutions for which they pay and distribute to their employees.

However, the key takeaway is that individuals become attached and will take software with them. If it is not on the preferred supplier list, then a champion or super-user/super-fan will advocate on your behalf to get it on there! Invaluable and efficient growth, right there…

o Wide and deep; you will be looking to land and expand in most, if not all, of your customers

Actions and outcomes from your research on Foundations and Beliefs

From your research you should end up with an assessment of the following:

• Is your C-Suite emotionally invested and committed to a Customer Success philosophy throughout the business?
• Is your culture supportive to deliver this philosophy?
• Are your customers seeing, feeling and achieving through this philosophy?
• Are your customers supporting you and your company to fuel the revenue growth engine?

You may have discovered that there are gaps in the foundations and beliefs at your company. This is unsurprising; not many companies have it watertight, just yet. Take heart and proceed!

Most companies have the best intentions and therefore, together, you will be able to make a difference to the way your company does business and have a positive impact on your customers and their businesses too.

The important people to identify as being truly customer-centric are your CEO and any advisors who exercise the most influence with them.

As with all data and research, you will need to keep up to date and ensure you are aware of any changes in personnel, particularly if they will have strong influence and have not shown a strong customer focus to date.

What do you do if you discover that these key players are not customer-centric?

This is a tricky situation to be in.

I have heard many situations where this is the case and usually they fall into a couple of categories. Similar to the early days of new technologies, you have early adopters (they are the pioneers, like you!), the adopters (follow when it's safer to do so and have a guide) and the laggards (they may or may not follow, after an extended time period due to lack of understanding, wilful or otherwise!).

Adopters

There are definitely CEOs and other company officers who really want the best for their customers, their teams and their business so while your investigations may lead you to believe that they are far away from the destination, it may still be an exceptional journey with amazing rewards.

You will need a commitment from senior management that they support you, will invest in you and in Customer Success and will act on your recommendations to transition to a fully-committed customer-focused philosophy imbued through the whole organisation.

While change can be slow to take effect, and there is reason to follow a measured approach to a fundamental project such as this, it will become obvious very early on if the C-Suite are only paying lip service to the implementation of true Customer Success.

If you are continually battling the beliefs of the key influencing officers and they are withholding investment, both in finances and their time, then it is time to consider that they may fall into the second category...

Laggards

This is a complex position to be in. If you're successful in converting these officers into adopters, you will have triumphed in a very harsh environment and your skills will be second-to-none – like reaching the summit of Mount Everest or completing an expedition to the heart of Antarctica!

Like these expeditions, it is not for the faint-hearted or without unexpected perils. I mentioned earlier that some Customer Success teams have been completely cut from a business and this can be one of the reasons for this happening.

You will need to be pushing for investment and change continually and demonstrating the impact you are having in concrete terms.

The learning you will gather from such an experience, whether it is successful or not, will also be invaluable.

However, I know of many examples of Customer Success leaders moving from organisations where they are just not ready to embrace this movement of business change. Their time will come, but for the Customer Success professional, they have preferred to move to an environment where they can guide and coach teams who are ready to go the full distance.

The choice is yours and either route will be rewarding, in its own way. This is a crucial element to your success within any organisation so it's best to understand as early as you are able exactly which route you are choosing so you can be best equipped.

Pioneer's round-up!

Key learnings

❖ A true customer-centric focus requires a demonstrable, top-down adoption approach
  - ❑ The whole C-Suite must be 100% invested and committed in putting the customer first

❖ Customer Success should have a seat at the table and the right to veto during the sales process, to ensure that the product is sold to fit-for-purpose customers
  - ❑ This will support the efficient and effective retention and growth of successful customers
  - ❑ Selling to the wrong customers, purely to hit a Sales target number, will incur a huge cost to the company as they will churn and potentially provide damaging testimony

❖ Remember that there are no longer such processes as pre- and post-sales; we are in a period of continual customer engagement
  - ❑ Each interaction will have an impact on the retention and growth of predictable recurring revenue

❖ True commitment to customer-centricity and Customer Success will ensure that each new idea will be tested to ensure it will have a positive impact on the customer lifecycle and experience

Actions

❖ Create and agree your mission, vision and objectives for your Customer Success function

❑ Consider the role of Customer Success at each significant customer milestone

❖ Review company documents, policies and processes to understand the priority of the customer in your company's approach

❖ Talk to and observe the actions of your C-Suite, colleagues and peers to ensure all customer-focused activities are being carried out as intended and are a priority

❑ Walk the walk vs talk the talk

Hot tips

❖ Involve your stakeholders in your research and thinking; if they join you on your journey, they will be more invested

***

For more ideas and templates, download the companion workbook at www.thecspioneer.com/resources/workbook

Get in touch to share your thoughts, questions, challenges and triumphs: talk@thecspioneer.com

1.3 Planning for Implementation

1.3.1 Data! Data! Data!

> Things get done only if the data we gather can inform and inspire those in a position to make [a] difference
>
> *Mike Schmoker (Author: Results)*

> It is a capital mistake to theorize before one has data
>
> *Sherlock Holmes/Arthur Conan Doyle*

Data is important for every business, organisation, function, programme and decision.

In Customer Success, you will need to know or plan to know many things:

- Who your customers are and something about them before you can meet them
- How to prioritise which customers with whom to engage and how
- Whether your product is being used, including which parts of it and whether customers understand the parts of the service which would help them most
- The trends of usage; are they seasonal or cyclical in any way?
- How to identify and have visibility of the warning signs for churn
- Create and communicate a programme into which everyone will invest and trust

- The ability to be able to track the effectiveness of all customer related activity so you can amend and adapt in a meaningful, proactive and efficient manner
- How to demonstrate value and outcomes to your customers, C-Suite, company and your team

Of course, the expectation is that when you're hired to look after customers, you will pick up the phone to them or go on site to visit them. And you should. You're expected to be fully employed with that activity alone. However, it is important that you maximise the use and impact of your time.

My assertion to my senior management team was this:

How can I be the most impactful with the limited resources I have and create the best client relationships without the data and analysis to help me make informed decisions?

> The goal is to turn data into information, and information into insight
>
> *Carly Fiorina, Former CEO of Hewlett Packard*

Data is crucial to any business, any individual and any leader to ensure decisions are made on an informed basis rather than taking a proverbial shot in the dark and hoping for the best!

Make informed decisions

> Any powerful idea is absolutely fascinating and absolutely useless until we choose to use it
>
> *Richard Bach, Author*

Data helps you make informed decisions: you have been collecting data through the activities discussed so far in this book. You have taken stock of all the current data held about your customers and your company's belief system. Putting in place a data collection process will help you present this data and track the impact of any processes or changes you apply going forwards.

It will also help you in your quest for creating a proactive, rather than reactive process.

Research and understanding are useful; it is the taking of action based on that data which is of vital importance. Otherwise, you are creating busy work for you and your team without the value of action and desired outcomes.

Translate findings into ongoing analysis and review

As with any project or undertaking, it is recommended to consider what you need, and to start small. Create a process and collect only that data which will be valuable to you.

It is always wise to start small, prove the theory and then build upon it. This is why the DIME cycle is a cycle and the final stage of any iteration is a reminder to EVOLVE that which has come before.

Remember then, when you are considering the content below, ask yourself the tough questions to ensure you are maintaining clarity about the objective and rein yourself in from trying to create an unwieldy monster.

What would the ideal data process include? Which data would you be able to collect? How, where and to whom would you present it? What would be the objective?

Here are just some of the data and uses which you may want to consider:

- Usage data
- Impact of processes, programme and any changes/evolutions
- Timely iteration/evolution
- Business Reviews
  - Internally
  - Externally
- Account planning
  - CSMs
  - Sales
  - C-Suite
- Risk assessment/Customer Health
- Early Warning System (EWS)
- Demonstration of value
  - Internally
  - Externally
- Justification for investment in technology and team

What data do you need and for what purpose?

Draw up your wish list, based on the investigations you have carried out. What will give you maximum visibility of your function's goals, targets, progress and priorities?

As you further complete your schedule of data, ensure you attribute the data with:

- Whose responsibility it will be to own, manage and provide the data
- To whom and how will it be delivered

- Which objective will it be fulfilling (refer to previous section)
  - e.g. To prove customer outcomes, usage and adoption, process improvements
- Short-term, medium-term, long-term requirement

While you may have written a wish list of data out of your requirements, remember to have a short-term, medium-term and longer-term goal in mind. This list should be as complete as possible, for what you know today. However, you will continue to add to this schedule and your longer-term requirements as you learn what works for your customers and your company. The DIME cycle is iterative so we will evolve our requirements for each branch of our mission as we come to it.

Therefore, some of your schedule will be filled with placeholders and this is ok. Relax and move on to the next step.

Ensure your immediate requirements and data have been identified, ownership and responsibility assigned and understand where the gaps may be and what to do about that.

What can you get and from where will it come

Invariably, and particularly in the early days of a product, whether in a start-up or an established traditional software company, we are not used to being able to capture user/usage data. I've heard many stories of product teams ignoring this aspect of the development, concentrating purely on features and functions which will be visible to the customer and which are cool and funky to build and deliver!

I would always recommend looking at what you want/need for the ideal tracking system before then looking at what you can get. This expands your thinking about the art of the possible rather than being constrained by what exists and therefore wondering 'what can I do with what I've got?'

This approach gives you a goal for which to aim and the understanding to allow you to devise a pragmatic solution in the meantime.

To allow you to focus and to maintain an eye on the long-term aim, write down your version of the ultimate goal (which will alter over time so remember to revisit this plan at each iteration) and now work towards your interim solution with those people you've identified as being your partners in this endeavour.

As with your earlier research, you will understand that there are many sources from which to gather the relevant data and here are a few to give you some guidance:

- Customer Relationship Management system
  - Do your Sales team use a CRM?
  - Is it a third-party tool, Excel, home-grown?
  - How are you able to access it?
  - Can you house your data and reporting in the same place to make pooling and use of data more centralised?
  - Do you want to use the same tool or do you need something more fit for purpose?
  - Is there a data warehouse which could be extended to include the data you need, if it's not already housed there? (see later section on 'Where to house the data')
- Product data
  - Does product data exist already?
  - What happens to this? Does anyone use and report on it already?

- How can you access and use it?
- Do you have authority to request developments?
- Will you be tied to product update cycles and resourcing constraints?
- Customer data
  - Gathering of Net Promoter Score (NPS) and customer satisfaction sentiment
  - Surveys
  - Anecdotal evidence
  - From the horse's mouth
  - Meetings, emails, phone calls, user groups, community
- Support data
  - Number of calls
  - Date of last calls
  - Severity of calls
  - Call category
  - Frequency of calls
- Training data
  - Onboarding feedback, time to onboard
  - % of users trained, % of admin trained
  - Frequency of training
  - Inclusion in customer onboarding processes
  - Date and type of training held
  - Trajectory of type of training held
- Marketing
  - Customer marketing outputs
  - Surveys
  - Events

How to manage the gap between requirements and available data

Your Chief Information/Technology Officer (CIO/CTO) will be a key figure in your quest for data as this is where the manpower will exist to manage these gaps, at the very least from a process perspective.

In the schedule created earlier in this chapter, you will have assigned an attribute of ownership to each of your data requirements. These are the people with whom you will need to nurture exceptional working relationships and be able to negotiate the bridging of the gaps you have identified.

In the case of usage and adoption data, this is extremely difficult to monitor and prove without tracking in the product itself. If this already exists, this could be great news, as long as it is tracking the actions which you feel, the customer feels, or has actually been proven to add value or a significant contribution towards the desired outcomes.

As an example, when we were building our customer reporting to be shared with our customers, we consulted with a number of our key customers to identify the activities in the product which needed to be captured and, conversely, those which provided no value at all. Scrolling, for example, showed that a user was physically in the system – that was activity, for sure but were they *gaining value* from that action or were they just navigating to the piece of information which would give them that value?

Through an extensive exercise, involving our customers, we identified the valuable actions and included only those in our customer reporting so that we could be transparent and confident in the activity and value each user was gaining from their use of the service.

Identify the actions which drive the outcomes your customers are seeking and ensure they are being tracked and reported.

The Product Manager and the control of the product roadmap will be important in understanding this data and how to upgrade it, where necessary. There is always a conflict between the list of desired features and available scope in each release; and that's just for the customer-facing experience! There will, also, always be priority given to an important customer feature – particularly if it's tied to a big or pivotal sales deal.

Having a good relationship and having built up the value of Customer Success will help you add weight to your case here.

See also 3.3 Demonstrating Value

Caution. Due to the heavy reliance on the product team's resourcing and release cycle, it is worth assessing what needs to be in the product in terms of tracking and reporting and what can be held outside. If you need flexibility to adapt in the early days, it's worth creating a bespoke system over which you have control until you know exactly what you want and know that iterations will be more measured and can be accommodated within the product release cycle.

Prioritisation

Even as you're working towards building the best data system you can have to support your activities and decision-making, an interim process is a must. As highlighted earlier, there should be a longer-term vision which you can build in stages as well as an interim solution which will be possible from existing available data and which will give visibility of the customers and your priorities. Even if this is only contract data, it must be centralised, visible and accessible by all.

How you manage the portfolio and the data you need will change over time:

- Discuss options
- Consider maturity
  - Early days
  - Small number of customers; usually high value
  - Large number of customers; usually low value
  - As your customer portfolio evolves

Stakeholder support

Consider the list of stakeholders you created earlier and with whom, by now, you may already have had some discovery conversations.

What doors will data open for you? What conversations need to be had and will be easier, stronger and more productive with data?

See also 3.3 Demonstrating Value

In the previous section, we talked about having firm foundations and beliefs and what to do if your company needs some help in that area. Foundations need to be looked after and nurtured – have you heard of subsidence in buildings or tree roots becoming unearthed and unstable? Without due care and attention, the values and commitment to Customer Success may become shaky and you need to tend to these challenges as they arise, preferably before they arise.

This means you need to use the data you collect holistically – to help you run the team, establish and evolve your programme, to help your customers achieve their value and outcomes, to help your company prioritise their resources and to continually demonstrate the value that your team is bringing to the organisation.

Customer Success is still relatively new in the modern business world and many companies are yet to be convinced of its lasting value. Many will implement the function because they've heard others are doing so, because they've been told to by their VC investors and funding partners or because they think it might actually be beneficial for their revenue and profit lines.

However, if you and they haven't invested the time into understanding and establishing firm foundations, whichever reason triggered the original idea will soon crumble and get swept under the carpet and the whole team will be out of the door. There are many examples of large enterprise companies, especially, going through several cycles of this – e.g. Microsoft has had several aborted attempts at cultivating Customer Success. On the one hand, this is painful for everyone involved and hasn't delivered the benefits to the company or their customers, as yet. On the other hand, it provides us – the Customer Success pioneers – with some invaluable learning experiences we can all share.

- Establish firm foundations within the company values and belief system
- Ensure customer focus is at the heart of the company's ecosystem, especially the Senior Leadership Team (SLT)
- Continually demonstrate value to your team and your company as well as your customers
- Gather existing data and promote the evolution of data which helps these goals
- Monitor, assess and iterate your customer journey
- Monitor, assess and iterate your programme ensuring the customer outcomes are the core focus
- Customers must be engaged at all levels to gather as accurate a temperature gauge as possible
  - Sponsors
  - Champions
  - Decision-makers
  - Executives
    - Value driven by the service
    - Outcomes achieved

Data is crucial and at the foundation level for every one of these imperatives. Data is the nourishment the roots need in order to keep growing and multiplying.

Where to build the data framework

Once you have identified the data you want, the data you can get and its sources, you will want to consider how you will use it and the process for getting, analysing and reporting it.

As with understanding the requirements and objectives of your data collection and reporting process, you may want to consider an interim solution as well as a longer-term goal.

In my experience as an IT Systems consultant, there was always an element of reporting to every project. As we've already highlighted, it begs the question WHY would you collect all this data, if you're not going to REPORT on it.

This is another reason why paying attention to the data, from the very beginning, is also a key component to any project. And what we're doing here, creating and sustaining a successful Customer Success function, is a project. A big project, with many phases and iterations but simply put, it is still a project.

At some point, someone is going to ask: 'Is what we're doing/what we've done proving to be successful?'

Without the data and without a means of confidently processing and presenting that data, how will anyone ever know?

I would hazard a guess that, in the short term, if nothing exists already, then a starting point with MS Office, G-Suite or similar will suffice to test your proof of concept, your processes and the data on which you can get your hands.

You need data early so make sure you have a quick solution for this, even while you may also be triggering the process to put in place something more robust and long term.

It is sufficient to get data which is good enough for now, while you work on the longer-term solution!

In-house

Every office, no matter the maturity of the company, will have some technology available to allow the collection, tracking and analysis of data.

Ignoring all the snobbery around Excel (or G-Suite or similar), these user-enabled applications allow you to start collecting data a straightaway in an accessible, visible and flexible manner.

I would posit that this is a perfectly acceptable way to start your analysis, particularly while investigating how your programme will evolve. You will need flexibility to adapt your analysis and reporting and this is much easier to action while the reporting is in your control.

Recommendations for processes set up in this way:

- Maintain the documents in a centralised, shared network area
  - Use shared network drives on your internal network
  - Content Management software allows you to manage your documents in the cloud so you and your team can access it from anywhere, at any time
- Ensure everyone who needs access, does so via the shared network location and NEVER by copies of the document being sent to them
- Review the documents on a regular basis and ensure you transition to a more robust and stable environment before the Excel system becomes a memory-hungry, formula-busting monster!

Disadvantages

- It is far too easy for a formula to get corrupt, either by user error, file-size or a number of other issues, so the greater the size of your portfolio the higher the priority to get this important data into a more stable environment
- No matter how careful you are, someone will always take an offline copy of the documents and make a change. This throws out the integrity of the data: Who has the correct version of the truth at any given point?
- While Excel and MS Access are undoubtedly capable of significant complexity and size, they can quickly become unmanageable and change control is much harder to effect if the data is in the hands of the business function

For these reasons and I'm sure, a million others, I would always start with Excel (or similar) to develop my thinking and then work with the relevant team to get this transferred into a much more robust system and process.

It may well be that you're ahead of the curve in this matter or that you have some capacity in your IT function to help with creating something either in-product or at the back-end. After all, much of the data will hopefully be coming from the product itself (usage data).

Including the data within the product itself will support any reporting you plan to share with the customer and it will avoid some of the disadvantages mentioned above, as it will:

- Allow all data to be held in one single, centralised location
- Be subject to strict change controls and testing, minimising the opportunities for mismatched data, erroneous formulae and dubious version control

Considerations to bear in mind when discussing the options of holding data in the product may include:

- There are multiple data sources; does it make sense to bulk up the product with all the data, even if we're planning to share some of it with the customer?
- While strict version control is preferable to the dubious change management which is likely to exist with spreadsheets, tying yourself to the product release cycle might be a little too inflexible
- In addition, internal updates are most likely to be deferred to the next release, if any capacity challenges arise

Due to the existence of many sources, it may be worthwhile investigating the possibility of a data warehouse (DW) to collect all the data in one central, controlled location.

There may already be a data warehouse in existence so explore the possibilities that this could be expanded to include any additional data which you require to give you a complete 360° view of your customers and your progress in achieving success for them and you.

The same constraints may still exist here in terms of flexibility and association with the release cycle so remember to ask all the relevant questions to understand the pros and cons of each solution before you pledge your allegiance to your chosen one.

There are many impacts and dependencies when considering how and where you will house your data and deliver your process but I'm going to stop here before I completely geek out – I'm more passionate about the intricacies of data than I realised!

Existing systems

Whether you consider using spreadsheets, the product or a data warehouse, there is bound to be reporting elsewhere in the business, so find out who uses what and from where their data comes.

It is a bugbear of mine to have duplication of effort anywhere so pool your resources, processes and systems wherever you can.

Sales and Marketing are both bound to have a Customer Relationship Management system (CRM/CRMS) to keep track of their leads, account planning and deal progress. Can you engage with this process and develop it further for your needs, in Customer Success? After all, we're all working with the same customers, why have this information in several disparate systems?

At the very least, ensure that the flow of data all comes from the same place so that any one point of user intervention (i.e. data input) happens only once and is then delivered to each point of use/transformation.

We want to make the customer journey as seamless as possible and that has to start with making internal processes as efficient and complete as possible.

CSM technology

There is an increasing number of vendors who specialise in or are extending their functionality to include specific Customer Success management processes.

Gainsight, Totango and ChurnZero are just a few of the more established platforms and you'll find a link to a list, which is maintained by Mikael Blaisdell on the Customer Success Association website, in the Glossary and Resources section of this book.

In my early quest for data, I googled CSM technology as I knew I needed help to identify my customer priorities, the trends which would help me understand customer behaviour better and focus to make the most efficient and effective use of my days.

I identified a list of ten companies in the field at the time and narrowed down my search to three with whom I wanted to investigate their offering. This was in terms of features, functionality and most importantly for me, the project effort which would be required not only to implement their tool but prepare for this activity *and* for administration purposes afterwards.

As a lifetime consultant, I am brutally aware that implementing any change, particularly involving a piece of IT software, takes hard work and almost always takes more time and financial investment that your early investigations uncover.

All these companies will take you through a demonstration of their system, which will be all-singing and dancing. There is no doubt that you would be able to achieve the same result for your process. However you will need:

- A clear understanding of your own process and roadmap into the future
- The manpower to dedicate to preparing your own data for the implementation
- Dedicated resource to commit to the implementation project, for the duration of the project

- Administration resource to maintain the implementation and to develop it over time, in line with the evolution of your customer management and programming
- A clear and effective process to ensure the continued adoption and engagement with the system, to ensure all information is kept up to data and actions undertaken
  - We're in Customer Success, we know that the first hurdle to proving success is to get the users to use the system on a consistent and valuable basis!

At the time, purchasing and implementing a CSM tool would have been like using a sledgehammer to crack a nut. My team were too small for the size of investment required. I continue to review CSM technology and recommend Customer Success leaders and teams to adopt the appropriate technology when they are approaching their own tipping point.

This may not be the right move for you, right now, but keep your eye on it and ask for the investment ahead of the time you'll need it to allow for implementation and embedding.

Considerations for your decision

Whatever you decide, there is a key hiring decision to make. My very first hire, even in a small operation, would always be a CSM Analyst (CSM Operations). My argument for this is that you will always be inundated with tasks and activities from researching how to structure your team, programme and function to dealing hands-on with customers. You need help and support with the research and with making the data visible for you to make timely and prioritised decisions. You are not super-human. You cannot do everything alone. It takes a village. So, hire in a villager who knows how to give you what you need – data = sustenance, motivation and momentum.

See also 4.3 Team development

Data is supremely important and so having someone who is comfortable around data, nay, splashes joyfully and geekily in data is, in my opinion, the most comforting and valuable hire you can make.

In summary then, where you house and how you manage the data is up to you and will develop and improve over time. Each time you feel you need to review and assess your position, remember to look at some of these considerations to help you reach the right decision, for the point you are at:

- Draw out your options
- Research pros and cons of each option
- Enlist your partners
- Size of team
- Size of portfolio
- Length of time to implementation
- Resources available to implement
- Resources required to maintain over time
- Evolution over time

Reporting and presenting the data

> Numbers have an important story to tell. They rely on you to give them a clear and convincing voice.
>
> *Stephen Few, Author and*
> *Data Visualisation Consultant*

Reporting

Without an audience, a story has no voice. The importance of collecting data is doing something with it; through analysis, transforming it into information and delivering it as insight so that clear and effective decisions can be made.

See also 3.0 DIME cycle stage: Measure

The reporting needs to be clear, concise and fit for purpose so there will likely be different reports for different audiences and objectives.

Customer reporting

Each customer is always going to ask how they are doing; how you think they are doing and how they are doing compared to your other customers, particularly those in the same industry as them.

It is important to be transparent with your customers so that you build rapport and the trusted advisor partnership for which you're aiming.

As you share information with them, this helps your partnership make informed joint decisions which will aid the trajectory towards success. They will be able to share this information with their internal decision-makers and stakeholders, building further support for your company and product.

Demonstrating value

Whether you have a revenue number attached to your function or not, we are a pioneering discipline so the burden of proof is squarely on our shoulders for the time being. There will come a time when Customer Success will be as commonplace and revered as Sales, perhaps more so. Until then, we need to stay ahead of the curve by demonstrating the value we bring for everything we do.

Over time, particularly as we develop and evolve, the presence and value of Customer Success will be self-evident. However, there will always be a need to track our progress and strive to improve year on year. For this, we need data, information, reporting and insights.

Deliver the insight

As each story needs a voice, there also needs to be a channel through which it is communicated. Clearly, concisely, effectively and with timeliness.

For customer reporting, it might be your goal to have in-product, self-service reporting which gives the customer ownership and transparency every damn day.

Whether you have achieved this method of delivery or whether you are sharing reports via another distribution method; it's a really smart way to exchange updates whenever you undertake a check-in with your customer so everyone understands progress as well as hotspots requiring further action.

In addition to this, it is recommended to include some executive level reporting in the Business Review (BR/QBR/EBR) meeting which you should hold with your customers on a periodic basis.

See also 1.3.2 Define your programme for outcomes and success

Ensure, internally, you have forums to communicate your value and celebrate your successes widely. This may include and not be limited to:

- Management meetings
- Access to Senior Leadership Team meetings
- All-Hands/Town halls
- Company/Offsite days
- Training days

See also 1.3.2 Define your programme for outcomes and success
3.0 DIME cycle stage: Measure

Pioneer's round-up!

Key learnings

❖ Data allows you and the business to make informed decisions

❖ Supports your transition from reactive to proactive

❖ You MUST take action based on the results of analysing the collected data

❖ Collect the data which is necessary and of value to you
  ❑ DO NOT collect data for collection's sake

Actions

❖ Create your data collection requirements
  ❑ Understand your short/medium/long term goals
  ❑ Manage any requirements gap
  ❑ Assign attributes for categories and ownership of data
  ❑ Use your stakeholder partnerships to assign responsibility for providing data and platforms

❖ Understand how, where and when you will analyse and report the data
  ❑ Consider your groups of stakeholders (customers, colleagues, C-Suite, etc.)

❖ Identify and assess collection and reporting tools
  ❑ Understand the capabilities of existing systems
  ❑ Align and 'piggy-back' where possible; avoid creating disparate data universes
  ❑ Assess candidates for future development
    ▪ e.g. CSM technology, in-app tools etc.

Hot tips

❖ It is sufficient to get data which is good enough for now, while you work on the longer-term solution

❖ Conversely, think BIG for your long-term goals. Avoid being constrained in your vision by what you can gather today

❖ Every story needs a stage and a voice; collect, analyse and report on data from Day 1!

***

For more ideas and templates, download the companion workbook at www.thecspioneer.com/resources/workbook

Get in touch to share your thoughts, questions, challenges and triumphs: talk@thecspioneer.com

1.3.2 Define your programme for outcomes and success!

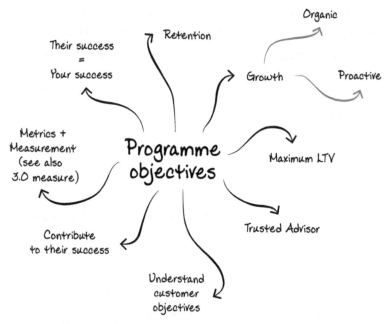

Figure 1.1: Programme objectives and concepts

Customer retention and growth

Customer retention

Most SaaS businesses will have a headline metric for customer retention, whether they have a formal Customer Success function or not.

A quick review of the data listed below will tell any management team if they have a serious churn problem. As the company and Customer Success team matures, the metrics will also reveal the growth rate and trend to ensure the implemented approach is the right one.

See also 3.0 DIME cycle stage: Measure

To start, here are a few of the more widely used headline terms and metrics to get your head around:

- **Annual/Quarterly/Monthly Recurring Revenue £**
  - o This is the monetary value of contracts due to renew in the given time period
  - o There are a number of ways to 'mask' the true value of this and, therefore, potential for masking a serious underlying churn issue.
  - o This can be calculated as Gross or Net, in the same way as the retention rates below
- **Gross Retention Rate %**
  - o This is the purest measure of customer retention
  - o It is usually the headline metric for most Customer Success teams; it's easy to understand as a percentage and comparable to industry benchmarks which are also expressed as a percentage
  - o Calculated using the recurring revenue £ value, as its base
  - o This should be the more pure, undiluted calculation as it measures like-to-like
    - ▪ Use the monetary value of all contracts due to renew in the given time period, deduct any contracts which do not renew, reduce by contracts which renew at a lower level than the original value (down-sell)
    - ▪ DO NOT take into account any increases in contract value. These transactions should be included in Net Retention/Net Recurring Revenue to show the new position (growth position)

- If upsell and cross-sell are included at this stage, the additional sales and growth could mask an underlying churn problem
- Due to these rules, Gross Retention Rate should never be more than 100%

- **Net Retention Rate %**
  - This calculation includes all transactions within an account; retention, upsell, cross-sell and down-sell
  - Ideally, this metric will always be above 100% as we want to ensure we are replacing any churn with expanding business within other products or other customers
  - A very healthy net retention rate would be 125%+; this would be considered to be a world-class position

    NB: No new customer accounts will be included in this calculation, only transactions within an existing customer

The metrics above are the headline metrics used by many in the Customer Success profession. However, there may be alternative sub-views. For example, for some companies, it is important to track the retention or churn of discrete customers and this can often be segmentation by Brand or Logo and would be measured and reported accordingly.

- **Logo/brand retention %**
  - This is a useful metric to understand whether you are retaining all your logos
  - As with other metrics, calculate the number of logos up for renewal in a particular period and compare to the number of logos retained at the end of the period

This may not have a monetary value assigned to it but the weight of the brands/logos will be instantly recognisable.

The brand/logo tracking can be part of the customer lifetime value analysis and predictions. This is often an activity undertaken by Sales, in collaboration with other teams within the organisation.

The metrics I have listed above are exclusively related to Retention and there are companies who measure and communicate in terms of churn. My perspective on this is that churn is from where our discipline arose.

However, I am a firm believer in focusing on the positive and we, as a discipline, should be looking at the positive aspects of retention, growth and achieving objectives, such as customer outcomes.

 Customer Success is about growth, sustainable growth and is the primary revenue accelerator for businesses today.

We want to cultivate lasting and productive relationships so let's focus on the motivating and proactive aspects.

Customer growth
Customer Success then, while its roots seemingly started with the challenge of churn, is now firmly focused on growth.

You may start your journey tackling churn, however, this is a short-term and reactive approach.

True Customer Success is focused on growth, first and foremost. What does growth mean, how do we achieve it for ourselves and for our customers, how do we measure it, how do we accelerate it and how do we communicate and demonstrate the value we're adding?

What do we need to be thinking about to get to faster and more efficient growth?

Organic growth
Organic growth is the main concept behind the knowledge that your existing customer portfolio is your accelerated growth engine.

We will always need sales teams to continue extending our customer portfolio, however the teams nurturing customers who have already signed on the dotted line will be making more of an impact in terms of being more efficient with time and financial investment.

Ensure the programme you design maximises the utilisation of your existing portfolio.

Your existing customers are your extended sales force. Use them. Train them. Make them successful. Convert them into promoters and advocates. Allow them to sell for you. Reap the benefits!

Here are a couple of other ways that your extended sales team will work for you:

Extend your reach into new teams
Working with your customers to ensure they get the most from your product and achieve their business goals is a great way

to ensure they become promoters and make noise within their company about your great offering.

Imagine, a sales team who has access to a fantastic sales enablement online service and it's assisted one of the team to close the biggest deal the company has ever seen. The team is one of ten within the business and the only one using the magic insight. Who else is going to want to get themselves some of those magic beans?

The other nine teams!! That's invaluable promotion and marketing for you, right there and your virtual sales team will be doing most of the work for you. This is a perfect opportunity to grow your customer portfolio by extending your reach within the company.

Organic growth through second order revenue

Have you ever heard how ivy, or any creeper variety, crawls silently and takes over every surface with which it comes into contact? Silent, determined and persistent. This is a real benefit of your virtual sales army. If you make your users unquestionably loyal to you and your service, they will take you with them. Every time they move roles, be that within their existing company or even more beneficially, when they move to a new company, they will take you with them. If you offer a one-user tariff, they will reactivate this in their new role. They will talk about you, to anyone who will listen and many who didn't think they were interested. And surely, they will ignite enthusiasm, desire and absolute need within their new team. They will introduce you and your physical sales team and Bob's your uncle!

Referrals and advocacy

Another channel for growth is through referrals and advocacy. Much like the Net Promoter Score query of 'would you recommend us to your colleagues and network?', this relies on your user base recommending you to their network. This may be at your request or of their own volition.

> Turning a customer into an advocate for your business is an ongoing journey. It is something that a customer success manager should continuously work on throughout the customer lifecycle. In order to maximise your advocacy potential, you need to foster the idea that at the end of the day, you will want to turn every one of your customers into passionate advocates for your business.
>
> *Irit Eizips, CCO & CEO, CSM Practice*

I've worked for companies before in which premium networking events are scheduled for prospects and existing customer champions. The intention, for these events, is for the existing customers to subliminally sell to their counterparts through the art of advocacy.

A more formal application of this type of selling is to request that your champion customers become reference sites for you to actively and openly use during your sales cycle.

Case studies are also invaluable as these demonstrate to any interested prospects real-life and demonstrable benefits, success and outcomes which they could implement for their own needs.

Maximising customer lifetime value

What does this mean?

Customer lifetime value is the amount of income you believe you would get from one customer over the lifetime of your relationship with them.

In a subscription economy, this is why we need Customer Success to focus on relationships and retaining and growing income.

We are no longer concentrating on one large contract with a customer, where the bulk of the money is paid upfront. We now need to ensure that a customer not only stays with us for many years but that their annual commitment to us grows over time to maximise the value they bring to us.

Imagine if a customer came on board with a contract for two years at £50k per year. Initially, that's a visible lifetime value of £100k. What are our options for extending that lifetime value?

- As a very first and basic step, we would want to renew the two-year contract for at least the same length of time again AND for the same value
- Ideally, we would want to extend the reach of the contract, in relation to the length of time AND the contract annual value
  - i.e. Increase the annual value to £100k instead of £50k
    - This is usually achieved by selling more seats or adding additional layers of the product to the contract which would increase the overall value
    - This is usually called 'Upsell'
- Even better would be the realisation of additional contracts within the organisation

- ○ Using your existing relationships and goodwill, you can identify other parts of the customer organisation which would benefit from your product
- ○ This is usually called 'Cross-sell'

CLTV = (Contract value + upsell + cross-sell) × No. of terms renewed

 The special part of this equation is that if the majority (or all) of your portfolio consists of growing companies, then the CLTV (and therefore your ARR) will continue to grow organically, *without your company ever having to sell to another new customer.*

Usage/adoption

A tell-tale indication that your customers (or at the very least, the end users of your product) are getting value from your service is a decent usage story.

If your product doesn't currently collect usage data, get this fixed asap! Work with your product team, explain the fundamental importance for them, for you, for the customer and for the company's ongoing viability.

It's also important to ensure that all areas of the product collect usage data so that you can understand which modules are being used, how they're being used and where possible how this is adding progress to achieving your customers' outcomes.

Tracking usage data is also one of the ways to identify risk accounts, as part of your early warning system (EWS) and your Customer Health evaluation.

For example, we all know that the quicker users adopt and find value in your product, the more likely they will become addicts and shout about the value to those who matter – the ones with the money to spend! One of the inputs to your analysis should be how long onboarding took – time-to-value is a crucial piece of data. Conversely, if you see a drop-off in usage, it is important to understand the trigger for this. Sometimes, it's perfectly explicable and expected. Oftentimes, it is a loud siren with accompanying flashing red lights to do something to save the account!

See also 3.2 Customer Health

While we're talking about usage data, it is worth noting that it is helpful for a number of reasons, not just as a means to starting to understand your chances of retaining a particular customer:

- Invaluable product feedback
  - Which areas of the service are being used well or perhaps in a different way to expected?
  - Which areas aren't being used? Is this because they are hidden, too complex or unnecessary?
- Enabler to enablement
  - Identify those features and benefits of the service which need better explaining and training (online, in-product or workshop)
  - Customer usage data and anecdotal feedback has often highlighted lateral ways to use the product to achieve

unusual or unexpected outcomes. This information can be exploited for additional growth

o Identify ways to work with your customer to apply change management principles within the implementation process

Customer satisfaction

Another focus for a Customer Success function and its programme are the considerations around the vibe of the customer:

- Are they using the product/service?
- Are they using the right modules of the service?
- Do they understand the depth, range and potential of the product?
- Are they satisfied?
- Are the expectations set during the sales cycle being met?
- How do they feel about the service?
- What sort of experience are they receiving and can it be improved?
- What are they saying about your service?
- What impact are your processes and touchpoints making?
- Are they spreading the love and getting you new and extended business?

We've all received the surveys, after a sale or after a visit to a website, perhaps after a successful finance/credit application. Love them or hate them, done well, they can provide you, as a business, with an invaluable view of your customer sentiment. We shouldn't be relying on guesswork or assumptions. We should be talking to the people who are using your service and find out how they really think and feel about it and you.

A few noteworthy tips:

- Engage with customer satisfaction surveys and processes ONLY if you plan to do something about the feedback. There is nothing worse than someone with a pain point being asked to share it and then getting nothing in return
  - How would that make you feel?
  - Make sure you have the buy-in of the Leadership Team and functional heads before you invest any time and energy in this!
  - Make sure you listen to the feedback and do something about it
- Make them short, meaningful and valuable to you and the customer
  - Time is precious to everyone; if you promise a survey will take mere seconds or one minute then you have more chance of getting a response
  - Equally, do you want to trawl through pages and pages of data to find the precious gems which will make a difference to your offerings, product, processes and growth rates?
- Time them well and for maximum benefit to you and your customer
  - I've heard many a tale of companies who trigger customer satisfaction surveys at just the 'right' time. For them. For example, just after a customer has successfully completed a credit application. Who wouldn't sing the praises of the process or institution which gave you cash when you needed it?!
  - This is a definite case of using the customer satisfaction survey process for vanity statistics purposes

- 'Vanity stats' are those headline numbers which you see on the shiny tweets, website banners and glossy one-page infographics which scream about their successes and achievements
- If you're going to invest time and energy in this process, do it to get a real flavour of how your customers feel by getting their feedback at arbitrary times during their lifecycle as well as choosing focal points such as:
  - End of the sales cycle
  - After a training session/workshop
  - Building up to the launch of a new feature
  - Sharing product roadmap and gathering suggestions for future releases
- If you're setting up surveys or NPS to gather customer sentiment, there is also good reason to time the data gathering in alignment with their renewal cycle
  - Ensure you give yourself time to do something about the feedback to help your customer feel successful before renewal time!

A customer satisfaction process can be incredibly useful in understanding how your customers really feel and what they need to stay loyal and advocates of your product and service. It can be delivered at scale using any of the numerous tools which now exist to help.

See also 3.2 Customer Health
4.2 Scale Customer Success

Importantly, you can and should also gather customer sentiment in person. This can be done at regular review meetings, it can be done at user events (e.g. meet-ups, conferences, community networking, user groups) and it can be done during periodic phone interviews.

We make assumptions about what a customer wants, needs and expects and if we don't sense check that periodically, we could find that we drift far apart and become stranded away from our customer base with no paddle with which to steer ourselves back to salvation.

Whether the expectations are realistic or unrealistic, miscommunicated or misunderstood, it is our responsibility to ensure we understand our portfolio to give us the best chance to fix any gaps and ensure we keep travelling in the same direction as our customers.

The only way to understand our customers is to talk to them – via online surveys, in-app feedback, telephone investigations, events, product user groups and scheduled meetings.

Talk to them.

Understand the feedback.

Act on it and publish your response.

Customer Success plan

I would propose that a Customer Success plan is crucial for every customer. It should hold the key agreements between the customer and yourself. It should also be a living document, in that you refer to it whenever you deliver something to or for the customer to ensure that you are adding value to the agreements made. At least annually, there should be a collaborative review of the document with the executive sponsor (amongst others) to assess progress and each party's commitment to their own actions and responsibilities.

These are some of the key objectives when creating your success plan framework:

- Can be held in-product, in CRM, in spreadsheet, in document
  - As long as it is easily accessible, visible and regularly reviewed and updated!
- Should be simple, easy to communicate, agree and understand
- Must be reviewed annually, at least
- Both parties must commit to their responsibilities to achieve the stated outcomes
- All parties must *agree* to the plan and be *held accountable*
- It is worth including change management principles within your Success plan; an implementation needs change management to have a chance at success and providing value

Here are some of the key components which many companies include in their Success plans. Inclusion of some items and even additional topics may depend on the size of the customer.

- Key contract information
  - Value, seats, renewal dates
- Reasons why the customer bought your product/service
- Agreed outcomes
- Agreed responsibilities
- Summary of journey to date and value achieved
- Projection for the future, to include account planning
- Customer reporting, at executive level
- Recommendations for maximising value
- Training plan

The intention is to use this as your partnership agreement and to involve the executive level sponsors at the customer, so keep the level of detail and focus fit for the purpose. Executive sponsors tend to have limited attention for detail and want to know the headline metrics, actions and requirements. If need be, have an Executive Summary and a more detailed section for the operational discussions you may have on a more regular basis.

You may also have picked up the idea that Customer Success is a two-way street and a partnership. This document and the Business Review meetings cement this way of thinking, not only for you but the customer too.

A partnership must have balance and your Customer Success plan will help you frame that with your customers, identify who has responsibility for which actions and ensure an agreement has been reached and the consequences discussed, for not fulfilling your responsibilities.

 You are helping them achieve their outcomes, they are not delegating their responsibility to you!

Product impact

Product teams are amazing and visionary which is how we have such choice and innovation in the market. This is also why there is such competition, and why we need to make sure that we are giving our customers what they want and need to achieve their business and personal objectives.

Ensuring your current product and future product roadmap combines the visionary aspects from your Product team and the absolute needs and requirements of your customers is key for any SaaS business to achieve the balance of innovation and customer retention and growth.

Innovation drives new potential for you and your customer and listening to your customers' goals and objectives will help drive that innovation in an aligned direction for maximum retention and growth.

A Customer Success team is likely to spend the most time with customers and therefore, will have the most opportunities to talk to users to discover what works well, what is challenging to use, what gives the best experience, what might be missing, what might be hard to find, as well as a whole plethora of additional insights from those who are using the product on a daily basis. This information gathering can also be incorporated into first-line support processes – online chat, support desk calls and email exchanges, etc. – and all contact points with the customer (e.g. CAB/User groups etc.).

Approach

The best piece of advice was given to me while I was sharing my 30- 60- 90-day plan with the C-Suite and my key stakeholders. I had undertaken the research activities and painstakingly unpicked our contracts so we had a complete and accurate view of our portfolio.

I had a better understanding of the shape and size of our portfolio and my plan was to meet all the customers so they had a contact point, and then once calm had been restored in their world, I would turn my attention to creating the framework, processes and collaborations required at our company.

One of my peers challenged me:

'Why are you waiting until month three before looking at process and framework?'

My response was one of complete surprise. Why would I not prioritise meeting with the customers and reassuring them that we cared and would work with them to achieve their required outcomes? Surely the goal was to communicate as swiftly as possible that we were committed to this partnership?

Their point, though?

What was I going to tell them to prove to them that we were now going to show up properly? More importantly, how was I going to ask for the support of key colleagues, if I couldn't articulate what I needed and when?

They had a very valid point.

This is how firefighting arises and persists.

This was the best advice I got in the early days: figure out the process and what you're asking of people. To get the support from your connected team, you will need to prioritise actions, resources and justify your requirements. Well-armed, you then make the ask, get people involved and demand results from others as well as yourself.

It is also really important to ensure you maximise every opportunity you get to interact with a customer. The more value you provide at each meeting, the more they will trust you and turn to you as an advisor and a long-term partnership.

Remember that this is an iterative process and it is important to start somewhere, with something well defined and communicated.

As part of a Design process, it is always useful to document the 'as-is' position to identify the activities which are being done well and those which are missing or need to be developed.

It is important to review key objectives before defining the 'to-be' process. We've discussed some of the potential programme objectives and concepts in the previous section and now is the time to understand what this looks like for you and your customers.

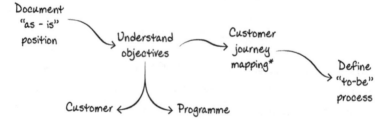

* See below for further details

Figure 1.2: Approach for programme design

Customer journey mapping

A customer journey mapping exercise is a flow-charting exercise undertaken from the expected perspective of the customer, e.g. What will bring them value? How will this engagement make them feel?

Using the output of your investigations so far, write down in sequential order, the touchpoints the customer has with your company:

- Pre-sales; what is the Sales process and who gets involved? What impact is there on the customer, how much time is involved and what information is gathered?
- Contract signature; this is an important milestone and involves a significant transition for the customer
  - Who is responsible?
  - What happens to the contract?
  - Is there a handover; what happens to all the valuable insight gathered during the sales discussions?
  - Who takes up the baton for the next steps?
  - Who holds ownership of the customer?
- Implementation/onboarding
  - Who is responsible?
  - If not CSM, does CSM get involved?
  - How long does it take?
  - How long should it take?
- Training
  - When does this happen?
  - Is there a roadmap for progression/certification?
  - Online/self-serve/onsite/public/bespoke
- Communications
  - How does the customer get contacted?

- ○ Automated processes?
- ○ How often?
- ○ Dedicated CSM?
- Driving outcomes
  - ○ What activities exist to drive outcomes?
- Renewals process
  - ○ Who is responsible?
  - ○ When does focus turn to renewal?
    - ▪ NB: Focus should *always* be on renewal!
  - ○ How is the relationship managed if there is someone other than the CSM handling this process?
- Expansion/referrals
  - ○ Who is responsible for this?
- Product upgrades/roadmap
  - ○ Is there a Customer Advisory Board (CAB)?
  - ○ Does a user group exist?
  - ○ How does the Product team interact with customers?
  - ○ How does product feedback from customers reach the Product team?
- Escalations
  - ○ Where does the customer go to report escalations?
- First-line support
  - ○ Is there a separate Support function?
  - ○ How and when do they escalate to the CSM?
  - ○ How does the CSM ensure a customer uses Support for the relevant calls and queries?

This is an idea of some of the touchpoints along the customer journey and no doubt you can add plenty more of your own to this list. There is a lot to think about and the main objective is that, to the customer, it looks and feels seamless.

The aim is to get to a customer journey, where all the relevant teams know for which parts they are responsible and the customer gets maximum value at each step of the journey.

The Customer Success Manager should be a main point of contact and an escalation point.

Remember, you are not solely responsible for the customer journey; each function and department plays its part so while you may propose and even own the master document/process, it is up to every team to map out the process and documents for their area. You are the master-weaver, bringing it all together.

With your contemporaries, consider which touchpoints are the 'Wow' or 'A-ha' moments for the customer. What will make them consider the product to be of utmost value to them, the service you provide to be second-to-none or that you understand their business as only a trusted advisor could?

It is these moments which will create the most stickiness (they will not be able to let you go) and therefore you should make sure you and the whole company maximises the benefit here. Make sure you *excel* at each of these moments in time.

'To be' process

Finally, we need to define the 'to be' process as this will be your Customer Success programme.

Out of the exercises in this book so far, you will be able to create the first iteration of your Customer Success programme and framework.

From this point, it will then be a simple next step to create a list of mini-projects which need to be completed, by the relevant team responsible, for each topic area.

What to include and how

There should be simplicity to your programme, as far as possible; the power is in how you deliver it and demonstrate value to your customers.

Major attention, particularly in the early days of Customer Success, is focused around usage and adoption. If they aren't using the service, there is little chance of you persuading their Financial Officers that this is money worth investing, and less chance that you'll be driving them to achieving their desired outcomes.

For this reason, your early programme design is likely to involve reporting on usage, identifying training needs and finding scalable ways of encouraging consistent usage.

See also 2.0 DIME cycle stage: Implement
4.0 DIME cycle stage: Evolve

 At the end of the design process, you should have a Customer Success programme definition. It should include:

- The customer journey mapping
  - o You may want an internal and external version of this, to assist communication to relevant parties
- An overview of the activities included in the Programme
  - o Customer Success plan
  - o In-product training
  - o Training plans
  - o Support
  - o Premium features

- Professional Services
- Coaching
- Bespoke training
- Customer contact rhythm
  - o Triggers, frequency
  - o What, when, where, how
  - o Who (both from your and their side)
- Success plan
  - o Organic and evolving document
  - o Updated at least annually
- Customer Reporting
  - o Usage/adoption
  - o Training
  - o Outcomes
  - o Value
  - o Return on Investment (RoI)
- Customer Community
- Events
  - o Conferences
  - o Networking
  - o Peer-to-peer learning
- Growth plan
- Business Review
  - o Frequency and delivery channel

See also 3.0 DIME cycle stage: Measure

Involve your key partners and stakeholders

Ensure you involve your key partners in the definition, creation and implementation of the Customer Success programme.

It is a far easier journey if you enlist people's support, rather than trying to dictate the approach, as you see it from your lone perspective.

 A great customer example of this is when we were transitioning from ad-hoc customer reporting to standardised reporting: the benefit to us was that it would be one single, automated process and the benefit to the customer would be that they would each get the same reporting. Up until then, only those curious customers got what they asked for, and it was unsustainable from their perspective as well as ours.

We needed something we could scale, something transparent, something we could benchmark and something which showed value.

One of our customer sponsors, at one of the top four traditional banks, was vocally displeased about current reporting and was convinced we were trying to hoodwink him about the value he and his users were getting from the service.

We invited him into a number of customer workshops, where we showed him behind the scenes and he got to provide input as to which actions provided value and which clouded the data. We also provided him with biscuits, so that could easily have been the reason he switched his tone when talking about the new reports.

Those customers involved in this process appreciated their inclusion in the project and this meant that they not only accepted and trusted the reports, they trusted us. They also became much louder proponents of our service for any potential customers with whom they talked.

If you involve your customers and your internal teams, they will have much deeper clarity around the impact and importance of your programme and will actively volunteer to be involved and get things done. Ultimately, it will help embed the customer-focused ethos throughout the company.

Customer groups, communities and gathering feedback

As an extension of this, it is very simple to set up some customer groups and events and if you work hard to involve individuals in your programmes, you will find that your customers become your event and community leaders. Salesforce.com user groups are an excellent example of this.

- Creates value and trust
- Value and trust = loyalty

 Communities require a degree of dedication, in the early days, so this may be something you want to save for your first EVOLVE iteration or further down the line, once you have built up some committed champions!

Additionally, if you are going to include User Groups or Customer Advisory Boards in your programme, you need to ensure you will ACT on the output of these. For this, you will definitely need to involve and have explicit agreement from your Product team.

Roles and responsibilities

Through clarity, you avoid confusion.

Avoid duplication of effort and maximise efficiency and effectiveness.

Make a decision over who has primary responsibility for owning the customer. There is an argument here that there is no longer such a concept as pre-sales followed by post-sales; every department is always in a commercial relationship as the aim is to cultivate that partnership and encourage expansion and growth.

It is imperative during all discussions and at the end of the programme definition that you get agreement from all parties that the result of the DESIGN process is accepted by them all. This includes them committing to the roles and responsibilities to which they've been assigned.

Pioneer's round-up!

Key learnings

❖ A Customer Success programme definition needs to be based on the mission, vision and objectives of the CS function

❖ It is important to keep your programme and your metrics simple. It is enough to nominate a couple of key headline metrics such as NRR and GRR

    ❑ The capture and analysis of both will enable you to understand if there is an underlying retention issue

❖ A Customer Success plan for each customer is key to ensure that all stakeholders (including the customer) understand and agree their responsibilities and the role they play

❖ Feedback schemes are a key component to your overall programme to track and measure effectiveness and levels of success

    ❑ Product feedback/Customer Satisfaction/NPS etc.

Actions

❖ Define and document the customer journey, 'as-is' and 'to-be'

❖ Incorporate your objectives into the programme definition

    ❑ Adoption

    ❑ Retention and Growth

    ❑ Loyalty, Referrals and Advocacy

❖ Understand the key headline metrics against which you will measure your programme
❖ Design your Customer Success plan and Business Review process for each category of customer
   ❑ Consider the Engagement model for each category of customer
      ▪ Remote/F2F/Groups/Conferences/Frequency

See also 2.2 Portfolio management
         4.2 Scale Customer Success

Hot tips
❖ The customer journey mapping = your approach and process
❖ Involve customers and key partners in the definition process; this will provide increased understanding, clarity and motivation to work in alignment with you
❖ Ensure you obtain AGREEMENT from all stakeholders for the design of the programme, their responsibilities and the role they play in achieving success

***

For more ideas and templates, download the companion workbook at www.thecspioneer.com/resources/workbook

Get in touch to share your thoughts, questions, challenges and triumphs: talk@thecspioneer.com

2.0 DIME cycle stage: Implement

Communicating and committing to the plan for the journey

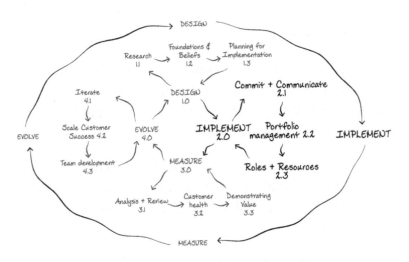

2.1 Commit and communicate

This is a period of change, and every process and programme – particularly one built on creating lasting relationships – involves individuals. It is well documented that we find change challenging; there are whole business functions dedicated to figuring out how to effect change most seamlessly.

It can absolutely be achieved and achieved well but it will need your attention, and that of the key stakeholders within your business *and at your customers.*

After all, we know that one of the major indicators of a failing project is a lack of adoption. A lot of Customer Success programmes are based on driving usage and consistent adoption, as a foundational route, to deliver the outcomes and success for which we're looking.

This is the same when we consider our desired outcomes for implementing a Customer Success programme and philosophy. We are committing to effect the change of implementing consistent and sustainable customer focus.

At a previous company, we used to tell our customers and partners that we drank our own champagne. We demonstrated the adoption, activities and outcomes into which our customers were buying.

This needs to be the approach to implementing any change. It should be much more than a mere ceremonial adoption.

A ceremonial adoption is one where a figurehead merely states that something new will be adopted and there is no follow-through. I'm sure we've all witnessed that as our customers promise to back the implementation of your product and you wait, with bated breath… for… nothing.

A ceremonial adoption contains empty words and empty gestures. This type of adoption is common due to 'peer' pressure encouraging managers to say they are embracing the newest way of doing something but not actually understanding what the implications, impacts or requirements are to get it done.

This position is understandable and familiar for many of us.

We know we are in a period of significant business flux and we, as Customer Success professionals and pioneers, are in a position to create and drive a seismic impact. We can help our leaders as well as those in our customers' organisations.

As well as motivating and driving our own business to surge forward in this transitional period, we can use our internal experiences and learnings to drive and effect transformational change for our customers.

How do you avoid a ceremonial adoption and pass on your learnings to your customers?

Many of the activities you include in your programme will be relevant and necessary for your internal communication and commitment. It is imperative – to avoid a ceremonial adoption – that you launch the programme well and continue to keep a focus on keeping it high in mind and it becomes the de facto way of life.

You must ensure that you, your team, your management and your customers are all willing to commit to their responsibilities in making your vision a reality.

Commit

During your research and design undertakings, you will have been working with a number of key stakeholders, internal and external with whom you will have discussed the plans for the future.

During these discussions, you will have heard their opinions, agreed to the journey ahead and the planned approach. At the end of the DESIGN stage, we recommended that *agreement* is key.

Each party must fully understand the programme, the vision and the part they play in it. They must be aware of all the key facets, dependencies and impacts. They must understand the ramifications of failing to deliver on their responsibilities.

Once all this has been ascertained, they must *agree* to the plan and framework. They must *agree* to fulfil their responsibilities as defined. They must *agree* to promote the programme and the ways of working to ensure your customer outcomes are achieved.

 Involvement and agreement are the first steps to commitment.

They are also *only* the first steps to commitment. There needs to be follow-through, from all those involved. Part of the agreement needs to be to communicate regularly and effectively to motivate and support the entire company towards its goal.

Communicate

You will have started the communication around your mission, vision and programme during the DESIGN stage of this process. Building solid relationships and understanding who your champions and advocates are will have been invaluable for creating a strong foundation.

It is worth making a fuss and fanfare about the official launch of your programme. In this way, it might look like a ceremonial adoption (all talk and no trousers) and it's up to you to ensure your network of champions do their job, spread the passion and cultivate a culture of true customer focus and success.

It is not enough to get the CEO or a suitable figurehead to make the announcement and encourage your colleagues to embrace the new and improved way of working.

There needs to be regular, prominent and effective communication. From all levels of the business.

If you managed to involve key colleagues in the research and design phases, you will have invested individuals with whom you can work to draw in the remaining members of all teams.

When the time comes, communicate to the same set of stakeholders with whom you consulted during the DESIGN stage

- C-Suite
- Managers
- Frontline/Field
- Representatives from other departments
- Customers

- If there are already too many customers in your portfolio, it would be sensible to create a focus group or pick a representative sample from the portfolio. In either case, ensure it is representative of the entire portfolio rather than just one type or size of customer

Use these people to maximum effect.

Review your programme and consider the change management activities you will highlight and propose to your customers. Utilise, test and report back to your customers on how effective these methods can be!

- Involve people of influence
- Create champions and advocates
- Create simple and effective processes that really make people's life easier!
- Train the trainer
- Explain the impact and outcomes
- Provide updates
- Show impact
- Address the needs of the personality types (A-type etc.)
- Consider gamification and incentives
  - How do compensation plans fit in? **See also** 2.3 Roles and resources and 4.3 Team development
  - Gamify using leader boards and badges
  - Use incentives and SPIFFs
- Create internal case studies

These are all ways to communicate your programme continually, every day and through many channels. Out of sight, in the business world, can mean out of mind so make sure you find clever and innovative ways to keep Customer Success at the top of everyone's mind and agenda.

- Posters on the walls
- Process diagrams
- Key Performance Indicators (KPI) on monitors around the office
- Informal 'award' days, periodically
- Visible leader boards

 Make it fun and engaging!

Another important component to this communication and commitment is to clearly demonstrate the value of your programme and the encompassing customer philosophy.

See also 3.3 Demonstrating Value

This will further enhance the commitment and investment in the programme and the company's customer-centric philosophy.

Motivate

Your communication should be designed to motivate others to embrace, adopt and fulfil the programme and the inherent customer focus. This motivation will drive the achievement of customer outcomes, renewals, expansion and business transformation.

This is crucial for both your internal partners and your customers. If they understand the impact of what they are doing and sometimes, more importantly, what they are NOT doing, this can motivate them towards doing the right thing. Every time.

Equally, if you find ways to make your customers understand the impact of what your partnership is doing for their business transformation and outcomes, they will stay with you and promote your successes to those in their extended network – becoming your virtual sales team members.

Pilot

A pilot can be a useful tool to achieve the goals of involvement, understanding and motivation.

Pilots are oftentimes used in sales cycles and in project implementations. It allows the team to run a small, focused test of the process to ensure that it is aligned to the correct outcomes and that the effectiveness and value can be measured.

If you already run pilots or proofs of concept (POCs) within your sales cycle or perhaps during implementation or onboarding of the customer, ensure that data and information being collected during these activities is retained, analysed and utilised for all the relevant purposes:

- Customer proof of concept
- Pilot the process, effectiveness and value
- Motivate everyone involved
- Adapt the process and programme, where necessary
- Measure value

- Secure further investment and commitment from customers, management and colleagues

On top of any pilot activities which may already be part of the operating rhythm, it is worth considering whether, when and how to utilise the pilot mechanism to measure the impact of the component parts of your programme.

I have spoken with a number of companies, who have either started their programmes by implementing component by component or by testing each component further down the line after implementation (this can be undertaken as part of the EVOLVE stage of the DIME cycle), to ensure the impact and outcomes for each is as anticipated.

This is a tried and tested project and change management methodology. When we attempt to implement or change everything all at once, it tends to become unmanageable and much more challenging to identify the gaps or weaknesses in the process, should they exist.

A pilot also gives you the benefit of comparing the pilot subject with those which are maintained in the status quo, thereby explicitly demonstrating the value of the tested process to those involved. If the value is not demonstrated, then adjustments can be made and done so in a timely and effective manner. Due to the focused nature of the rollout, there will be minimal costs associated with a process which may need adjusting. It allows for fine tuning, in the most cost-efficient way.

The aim is to demonstrate to others the value of what they have achieved and the heights to which they can aspire, in a clear and focused manner. A pilot is a superb way to test and prove this. Involve people and they will understand. And be motivated!

Deliver and adapt

While there are two more stages in the DIME cycle, it is recommended, as suggested by the pilot activity above, that delivery of any phase of the programme should be monitored and adapted where tweaks are required. This speaks to the concept of applying DIME at the micro and the macro levels. The EVOLVE stage is much more concerned with developing the programme to the next attainment level, rather than ensuring that the current iteration is being implemented smoothly.

See also Part I: How to use this book

How can we deliver this version of the programme effectively and encourage full adoption versus the ceremonial state?

The programme definition, as discussed, should be clear, simple and easy to consume. The next level of detail, then, includes the processes and activities which will need to be put into play to achieve the programme objectives.

Effective and efficient processes

We need to choose manageable steps to take, one after another, to wend our way to the destination of success.

The steps may be taken in quick succession and iterated as required but should be as clear, concise and focused at each step as possible.

To begin your implementation, define a simple process and educate everyone on their responsibilities and how and when to provide feedback to ensure the process is aligned to the programme and objectives.

Once the process is proven to be effective, you may develop where it has been shown that it will add value, otherwise leave well alone until you need to make a step change in the evolution of your programme; this might be due to the increasing size or shape of your portfolio, the drawing down of investment capital or any number of other scenarios.

Essentially, you will evolve and develop as you learn and as your product and customer evolves and matures. You will mature at the pace which makes most sense to you.

Consistency
The programme and the process will provide consistency and a benchmark by which customers and colleagues will be aligned to their success outcomes.

This will help the programme be as effective as possible to allow maximum resource dedicated to valuable customer conversations and outcome delivery.

Consistency will also help you to scale, if you need to, now and most definitely into the future as your business and portfolio grow.

Tracking and feedback
We discussed that data is crucial, in any business and particularly when you're implementing business transformation.

Ensure that you have the basics in place for the implementation stage of your programme. Whether you apply the pilot principle or go Big Bang, you will need data to understand the impact and outcomes of your new processes.

It is also important to provide a feedback route; how will people advise the experience they are now receiving? How will your colleagues propose tweaks and improvements?

The inputs at this stage form part of and will be useful during the MEASURE stage of the cycle.

Technology

To begin with, I would recommend proving your programme with the tools you have to hand and keeping it as simple and familiar as possible. This will help with validating that the process is the right one, with the added benefit that you're more likely to get adoption if the team are using tools with which they already have experience.

I would, however, also recommend that you keep an eye on the market to see what's available, what are the capabilities and to understand where your tipping point might be to adopt some more advanced and specialised technology. You want to find the right time to begin the project so that implementation will coincide with the need for the advanced capabilities. This can be a tricky balance to find!

Recommendations for the implementation of specific CSM technology:

- Embrace at the right time; IT projects soak up time, investment and people
- Automation can help enormously, if done well
  - Can be a distraction if done badly
  - Can be a turn-off for customers if not well thought through. Do it because you know it's right, rather than because everyone else is doing it…

- Tracking and prioritisation
  - o At the tipping point of customer portfolio size vs team size, you will need automation

Targets

Change takes time and this is a fundamental shift to implement, so you need to track the impact and be pragmatic about the goals you set, for each small step change you plan to make, even though you should also be ambitious with your mission, vision and ultimate impact.

The key point to remember here is to set some targets, even if they are very rudimentary. At the early stages, I would recommend they are simple and basic so that they don't distract from your primary focus. Over time, which may be months and up to a couple of years, your targets and tracking will become much more sophisticated as they evolve based on true understanding and on the outputs of your programme.

Some of the targets may even be related to the shape and speed of your rollout and the next projects on which you want to concentrate.

For example, the growth of your team and the way that you segment and manage your portfolio are inherently connected to the success of the programme.

As your programme becomes much more proactive than reactive, your customers will gain much more value and your retention rates will stabilise (and net retention will increase). This will allow the company to invest in the Customer Success function to give maximum support to their business growth ambitions.

Businesses are beginning to understand and vocalise the importance of recognising and utilising their customers as their most important revenue generator. One of the fastest growing SaaS companies has recently been quoted as stating:

> When we're a multi hundred million-dollar ARR company 2 years from now, one of the top reasons will be because we invested in Customer Success early.

You're on your way to joining them as you communicate, commit to and motivate everyone to embrace and deliver on your Customer Success mission. This will allow you to transition from reactive to proactive and utilise your most precious asset – your customer – as your revenue growth engine.

Pioneer's round-up!

Key learnings
- ❖ Implementation needs proactive commitment and communication. From everyone
- ❖ Full comprehension of key components, dependencies and impacts is key to commitment and effective communication which ultimately will lead to successful implementation
- ❖ Regular and effective communication, including feedback and follow-up, is fundamental to successful adoption
- ❖ The strong connections you have nurtured with your peers and stakeholders are invaluable to the success of implementation and adoption

Actions
- ❖ Communicate regularly and effectively; people consume information and are motivated in different ways
  - ❑ Be creative. Make it fun and engaging!
- ❖ Find champions, within your partner and stakeholder network, to support, spread and evolve your communication and adoption strategy
- ❖ Set targets to allow you to track and monitor progress
  - ❑ Ensure you provide feedback channels and always follow up on actions and suggestions
- ❖ Design simple processes which will be effective, efficient, easy to use and facilitate the adoption of your programme and its activities

Hot tips

❖ Involvement and agreement at the Design stage are the first steps to commitment
  ❑ Ensure this step is fully undertaken and understood, to avoid a ceremonial adoption
❖ Use your programme adoption/change management strategies to support your own implementation
  ❑ This will test your theories and show your customers that you drink your own champagne!

***

For more ideas and templates, download the companion workbook at www.thecspioneer.com/resources/workbook

Get in touch to share your thoughts, questions, challenges and triumphs: talk@thecspioneer.com

2.2 Portfolio management

Transition from reactive to proactive

The overall goal, regardless of how you have personally defined your vision, mission and programme, is to find a way to be as proactive and provide as much value to your customers, as possible. This will lead to them achieving their outcomes. And their success equals your success.

You may have been drawn to the concept of Customer Success because you currently have a churn challenge and/or you also live in a professional world where your days are dictated by customer demands, support calls and firefighting. Perhaps, you're already managing to be proactive, in some form. Whichever position you're currently in, the plan is to proactively manage and prioritise your customers to greatest impact and effect.

Your Support team should be fielding the incoming calls from customers needing to understand why something isn't working or not working the way they feel it should. Basic and repeated questions should be fielded by this team.

 When asked the difference between Customer Support and Customer Success, very often seasoned CSMs will offer a key differentiator as being:

Support = Reactive

Customer Success = Proactive

Customer Support works at a reactive and operational level and should be encouraged to handle all calls and enquiries of that nature.

This allows you and your team to analyse the portfolio and prioritise those customers which most need your focus and value.

In the early days, portfolio management may be reasonably light touch, particularly if you are a company with a small number of high value customers. At some stage, though, you are going to have too many to handle in your head or the capacity to give them all the same level of care and attention. It's hard to acknowledge, particularly if you're a natural nurturer. Pragmatically, it makes sense to give more to those who are more valuable.

 Each customer brings a different value, and portfolio management is about understanding the value, the balance and the time at which each of these becomes important.

A small customer may be low value in terms of ARR, but the brand may be of exponential importance so it might be key to elevate the status of this customer for strategic purposes.

All customers are important and should be given the best experience you are able to offer based on the investment you have and the cost of service and cost of retention to the business. Portfolio management also incorporates the concept of segmentation and each segment will have an appropriate level of engagement from your team and company.

These are generally categorised as:

- High-touch
- Medium-touch
- Low-touch
- Tech-touch

See also 4.2 Scale Customer Success

As a general rule, the segment within which a customer is categorised is rarely publicised outside your organisation. You want to ensure that each customer feels valued by you and this can be achieved using different engagement levels; indeed, some customers will prefer to have a tech-touch approach even if you would categorise them as a high-touch customer. A buzz-kill for a customer might be, though, that another customer has told them that they are deemed to be 'more' important than them.

Conversely, as with loyalty schemes (e.g. airline miles, supermarket rewards cards), it could be used as an incentive to grow the account and get an enhanced level of service/value from you.

For the purposes of implementation, we are going to concentrate on embracing the concept of being proactive and prioritising our customers based on the knowledge we currently have and the resources available.

You will need to have parameters in place to understand what needs doing when. This also comes much more into play as you expand the team, so everyone is applying the same care and consistency to the customers in their personal portfolio. This means that no matter who is looking after a customer (people go on leave, get sick and move on to other roles), the customer will always feel the same level of care from you, as a company. Consistency is key!

Another reason to consider your portfolio management and segmentation approach well in advance, is that it will inform your resourcing decisions as you consider how you will build and expand your team. The different engagement models require a different skill set from your team, although everyone will have an overall motivation towards making people successful. In simple terms of financial investment, too, you may need to decide between technology and manpower.

For example, if you have a largely tech-touch portfolio, you will need technology to automate the high volume of customer contact required.

See also 4.0 DIME cycle stage: Evolve

Determine focus and priorities

 Portfolio management is a framework within which to proactively and effectively prioritise your focus.

Define strategy

Your strategy, to begin with, may and should be as simple as possible, regardless of the size of your portfolio.

Keep it simple and track the value that you are providing to your customers for their outcomes and to your business retention and growth goals (i.e. use DIME at the micro level).

Perform cost vs benefit analysis on each activity to make sure they are achieving enough value. If they fail to meet your benchmarks, ditch them and find another to do a better job!

One size doesn't always fit all, so allow for a little flexibility, and with the right skills in your team and the business as a whole, you will be able to trust the judgement call of the individual who is responsible for each section of the portfolio.

In the beginning, you may apply the same base strategy to your whole portfolio, particularly if you are starting out with a small portfolio or if you're planning to adopt the pilot implementation approach (let's call this the proactive portion of your portfolio).

As you increase the proactive portion of the portfolio, you will find it hard to scale without the help of segmentation and a strategy for each. It is worth bearing this in mind when starting out so that you are conscious of how to manage any change in engagement level that a customer might experience in the future, i.e. a lower value customer may start as high-touch if that's the broad brush you use at the beginning of your portfolio management and then they may be moved to tech-touch. It can be hard to wean them off the more personal service they have been receiving and understandably so!

Conversely, if you have designed your programme well, with successful adoption strategies, automation and use of internal customer resources; you may be able to move customers seamlessly onto a lower touch model as they mature and become self-sufficient, on their journey with you.

 When considering your strategy, it is important to bring in the work you've done for the customer journey mapping exercise from earlier in the DESIGN stage. All these processes, maps, definitions and strategies should be adaptable and are expected to evolve as you move forward along your own journey.

Remember to adjust the customer journey with discoveries made during your IMPLEMENT stage.

Lifecycle planning
Define customer journey

- Pre-sales
- Sale/Signed contract
- Onboarding
- Training
- Adoption
- Growth

See also 1.3 Planning for Implementation (Customer Journey mapping)

Define lifecycle and growth triggers

- How and when will you get them to grow
- Triggers
- Objectives and targets
  - By segment?

Customer segmentation

If you work closely with your Sales team (and I would propose that this is a necessity to ensure alignment and a streamlined way of working), you are more than likely to have already come across customer segmentation. Most Sales teams segment their customers for a number of reasons

- Size of account
- Anticipated Lifetime Value (LTV)
- Power of Influence
- Brand/Logo
- Skills of team members
- Industry vertical
- Domain expertise

Does this exist at your company already?

As a starting point, it may make sense to mirror the segmentation that the Sales team has in place. This allows for the simplest approach to segmentation and full understanding and alignment for everyone involved. It would also allow for natural team collaboration between the Account Manager and the Customer Success Manager on the related accounts.

Another consideration might be the existing skills in your team, particularly at an early stage, if you have inherited the team or are drawing on existing skills within the company. When you have a resource constraint – headcount freeze, inherited staff, etc., it might be that the wisest way of segmenting your portfolio is by playing to your team's strengths without any hard and fast rules behind the decision.

See also 4.0 DIME cycle stage: Evolve

When should you start?
If you have a handful of customers and enough team and technological resource to manage this adeptly, then you can be very proactive right from the beginning without necessarily going through the formality of defining your segmentation.

However, in your mind at least, you will have applied some kind of informal segmentation and prioritisation.

I would formalise that, in a very simple form, as soon as possible. This will give you a starting point and visibility of how your portfolio is growing, This, in turn, will give you an indication of when you need to be thinking more seriously about how you segment your customers and the engagement approach you will apply to each.

How do you go about it?
Some of the criteria for segmentation are already used by Sales teams. It would be perfectly reasonable and make sense from a consistency and alignment perspective to adopt the same segmentation categories and criteria as your Sales team, particularly if you report into the Chief Revenue Officer (CRO).

- Logo
- Size of business
- Contract value

- Lifetime value (LTV)
- Combination of metrics; weighted?

As always, I would recommend keeping things simple so choose one key metric by which to segment and apply the engagement model you will apply for each.

Ensure you communicate this clearly within the organisation so customers are not promised a level of engagement which does not fit your framework.

For example, many Account Managers will argue that their first initial deal with a new customer warrants high-tough engagement as the expected LTV meets that specific criterion. Be clear about the boundaries and stick with them. Also, reassure your Account Manager colleagues that a customer can move between segments. It is much easier to increase the engagement with an account than to take it away.

Monitor Customer Health

We touched on Customer Health in our data chapter in terms of what it is and which types of data you might want to collect to formulate an overall picture of the customer and their status at any given time.

See also 1.3.1 Data! Data! Data!
3.2 Customer Health

What do we mean by Customer Health?

This is not the score, this is the overview of any given customer, at any time. It may be in the shape of a scorecard or whichever form makes sense to you and your company.

Gathered, reported and analysed well, this will give you an indication of how likely a customer is to renew, expand and refer your product to their network.

Be aware that you can do all the right things, record good data and feel that a customer is 'safe' or 'green' and inexplicably they churn. This has been termed the watermelon effect by Adam Joseph, Founder of CSM Insight & Director of Customer Success at Gainsight, and Matt Myszkowski, VP EMEA Customer Success at SAP. The customer may be emphatic in their positive position on your product but a decision is made to churn which was not foreseen by anyone, including your customer champion. Therefore, the account may look green on the outside but if you cut it open, it's red on the inside. Hence, the watermelon effect!

Customer Health and any calculated score, even including qualitative data, should not be wholly relied upon. This is a crucial reason to ensure that Business Reviews undertaken with any customer must include the final decision-makers for the renewal/expansion contract.

Proactive portfolio management will create the momentum for real customer growth through the process you create to push customers through their journey and lifecycle with you.

By managing them and their outcomes successfully, you will move them from their initial contract, through expansion in their own business, into referral champions which will lead to an exponential natural customer growth trajectory for you.

Lay the foundations firmly, pilot the process, alignment and value you are achieving and ensure every activity you and your team undertake provides absolute value to your customer ambitions and your own success.

Pioneer's round-up!

Key learnings

❖ Portfolio management supports the move from reactive to proactive programming
  - ❑ It allows you to deliver the greatest impact and value with the available time and resources
❖ The proactive management of your portfolio provides a set of parameters within which each of your CSMs can deliver alignment and consistency, with focus and priority
  - ❑ Segmentation rules should be applied as a base from which to start
  - ❑ CSMs should be empowered to be autonomous and flexible to deliver what is needed to each of their customers
❖ It is prudent, as a starting point, to utilise the same segmentation as the Sales team
  - ❑ This allows alignment, consistency and natural collaboration across the company

Actions

❖ Determine the focus and priorities for your portfolio management strategy
  - ❑ Whole portfolio or start with a pilot?
  - ❑ Same activities for all or segmentation from the start?
  - ❑ Growth plan
❖ Start simple. Track impact, value and effectiveness. Evolve

❑ Use DIME at the micro level
❖ Monitor your chosen metrics and Customer Health to ensure you are achieving, or at least moving towards, your desired goals

See also 3.2 Customer Health

Hot tips
❖ Each customer brings a different value, and portfolio management is about understanding the value, the balance and the time at which each of these becomes important
❖ Update the customer journey mapping as you learn from the implementation activities
❖ Empower your CSMs to be autonomous and flexible
  ❑ Consider that your contacts will have differing engagement preferences
    ▪ For example: millennials have a preference for mobile-first, in-app experiences with limited tolerance for meetings and face-to-face interactions

***

For more ideas and templates, download the companion workbook at www.thecspioneer.com/resources/workbook

Get in touch to share your thoughts, questions, challenges and triumphs: talk@thecspioneer.com

2.3 Roles and resources

No matter which company you're in or the size of it, if you're just beginning your journey into Customer Success, the chances are your team will be small.

With the right framework, measurement and demonstration of value, you will be able to direct investment to convert this situation into strong growth for the team and the programme.

Roles in Customer Success

There are plenty of ways to structure the Customer Success team. Companies currently and will continue to do this quite differently from each other. The crucial consideration is to figure out, over time and testing, what works best for you and your organisation, and remembering that this will change over time. This is fine and is all part of your EVOLVE stage and trusting yourself to the iteration process.

The core role would be the Customer Success Manager (CSM). This is the team member who is usually recruited first.

There are other roles which could be incorporated into a Customer Success function and at a minimum are complementary teams and mandatory collaborations

- Customer Success Manager
  - Skills will vary by portfolio segment
  - Skills will vary by portfolio objectives
- Customer Success Operations
  - Data analysis
  - Framework delivery
  - Quality assurance
- Onboarding

- Implementation
- Training
- Customer Support
- Consulting/Professional Services

The reporting structure may dictate which teams form each of your business functions. Some organisations have Customer Success reporting into the Chief Revenue Officer so that all revenue numbers are their responsibility. In this case, only CS and CS Operations would be within the Customer Success function. However, if the reporting line was into the Chief Operations Officer or if you have a Chief Customer Officer, then all the teams listed above are more likely to be found within the same reporting line.

Responsibilities

Ensure that the responsibilities, agreed during the DESIGN stage and communicated during the initial stages of the IMPLEMENT stage, are being delivered.

Identify any gaps and understand why they exist, whether they need a resolution and how to do this. Assess the impact and decide if this is something to be easily resolved now or create a project for this next evolution.

See also 4.0 DIME cycle stage: Evolve

It is the responsibility of everyone involved in the implementation, including the customers, to observe the process they are delivering and feed forward into the measurement and assessment of the results you are getting.

Those delivering and receiving the impacts of your framework are best placed to provide the feedback from the front line. Are the activities having the desired effect? Is adoption at the level to be expected for the lifecycle stage? Are we aligned to the business outcomes of our customers, delivering these activities?

Partnerships

Once again, partnerships are key to this stage in the cycle. The entire organisation has responsibility for ensuring that the customer-centric philosophy is a success, to achieve the exponential growth which can be delivered from our customer base.

We spent a lot of time identifying and nurturing those relationships from day/page one. Life is all about connections, they are the roots from which we grow and the stronger you have made your partnerships, the easier these stages will be.

 There is a great analogy applied to one of the ten laws of Customer Success which was co-ordinated by Gainsight and paraphrased here:

If you have two rowing boats in the middle of a lake, there will be a natural propensity to drift further and further apart, without any human intervention. Each boat needs to have an oarsman, determined to keep the boats together, aligned and moving in the right direction.

This is true of all partnerships, each party needs to have an 'oarsman' to keep the relationship aligned, to ensure that all the agreements which were established at the DESIGN stage are adhered to or adjustments made, in collaboration with each other to get to the same destination.

Each team within your business will have a key role and responsibility in the implementation and consistent delivery of your programme

- Sales
  - Contract details
  - Smooth handover of customer
  - Outcomes information
- Onboarding
  - Aligned with the CS methodology
  - Efficient and effective time-to-value
- Training
  - Proactive training plans
- Professional Services/Implementation
  - Efficient and effective time-to-value
  - Strategic outcomes alignment
- Customer Support
  - Reactive triage
  - Efficient problem resolution
  - First-line knowledge base and self-service

An objective for your programme resources should be to include your customers front and centre. They should be a key resource in each of your accounts by providing channels for self-service

- Train the trainer
- Super users
- Driving adoption
- Gamification and rewards (VIP events, badges, awards etc.)
- Knowledge Base
- Incorporation into Learning and Development frameworks
- Embedding into their processes
- Building community and network

Business Reviews

Another way to ensure you involve the customer is to hold Business Reviews with them. These are likely to be a mainstay of your entire programme; in time, you may refine the way they take place and the frequency, but during an implementation period, it's a useful route to the key players to ensure you have complete alignment with their business goals and outcomes as they specifically pertain to your product and service.

As we have highlighted in previous sections, it is important to get the highest-level stakeholders to these meetings. This, more than anything else, indicates that they are invested in your partnership. Time is precious to us all, and senior management give time sparingly!

- Key stakeholders should attend, and definitely someone who makes the financial decisions around renewing and expanding the use of your product
- Shows commitment on both sides
- Review the agreements made to deliver outcomes and success as a joint responsibility

- Ensures that each party has a reliable and determined 'oarsman'
- You need to design your Business Review process to provide impactful value so that the key stakeholders want to attend

> I know you have a lot to cover and you're excited to share your success with adoption, support resolution, or your new and exciting product roadmap... but seriously, if you want your executive sponsor to be excited about these quarterly meetings, you want to have a major mind shift and make this meeting about them. This means that the more open-ended questions you ask, the more you're going to be able to create an alignment between their business goals and needs to what your solution can offer. In other words, the more opportunity to increase the perception of value and hence the possibility of value realisation.
>
> *Irit Eizips, CCO & CEO, CSM Practice*

Through the careful and phased implementation stage, you will transition from reactive to proactive, ensuring the customer receives the best care and attention by the appropriate resource to lead them to their business outcomes and your exponential growth.

Through efficient processes and effective feedback mechanisms, you will provide inputs into your MEASURE and EVOLVE stages, which we will discuss in the next two sections of the book.

Pioneer's round-up!

Key learnings

❖ Roles and responsibilities must be defined and agreed during the DESIGN stage and then monitored during implementation to ensure they are being delivered and having the expected impact

❖ Business Reviews must be designed to maximise the impact for the time available

❑ To ensure that the key business stakeholders want to attend each time for the value they are receiving

Actions

❖ Consider the roles and responsibilities of your stakeholders, partners and customers

❑ Self-service

❑ Train the trainer

❑ Embedding into their processes

❑ Providing feedback and tracking from their internal systems

❖ Design your Business Reviews to ensure they are simple, effective, impactful and of value

❑ Easy to use for your team to update

❑ Easy to consume and action by your team and customers

❑ Of consummate value so stakeholders will always attend and actively participate

❖ Ensure all actions are documented, tracked and delivered by those assigned ownership and responsibility

Hot tips

❖ Evolution is key. Your structure will change over time. Be aware of this, embrace this fact and develop your roles, responsibilities and reporting lines, as necessary

❖ Partnerships are key. Ensure each 'boat' has its own oarsman, focused on keeping the boats moving together, in the same direction

***

For more ideas and templates, download the companion workbook at www.thecspioneer.com/resources/workbook

Get in touch to share your thoughts, questions, challenges and triumphs: talk@thecspioneer.com

3.0 DIME cycle stage: Measure

Reviewing, assessing and demonstrating progress

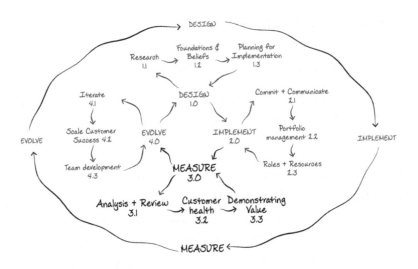

3.1 Analysis and review

Compare and contrast

With every programme and any business activity, there needs to be some form of measurement to assess the impact of the programme and to ensure the expected outcomes are being achieved.

It is very easy to get drawn into the firefighting, the reactive measures and even if you're being proactive, you're busy being proactive and getting in front of customers.

How do you know that your days of being busy are having an impact? And if they are, is it the right impact?

Baseline and benchmarking

What are you comparing? How will you know if you're making progress and heading in the right direction?

Creating a baseline and being aware of benchmarks – which can be set by you and/or gathered from external sources – is a great place to start.

I'm a huge fan of making connections and being part of a community. There's a supportive community enveloping the Customer Success discipline. We're all looking to share experiences and find the quickest route to success for our customers, our companies, our team and of course, ourselves.

There is a troop of CS pioneers who are sharing their thoughts, research and trends for the future. The internet, community pages, networking events, meet-ups and conferences are all great places to understand how to measure, baseline and benchmark your programme, team, philosophy and function.

When I started out in Customer Success, the first thing I did was research for online communities and in-person events so that I could learn from others. There wasn't much around at the time, in the UK, so those of us who found each other, created our own meet-ups and community.

Global communities and conferences will help but it's also always super helpful to find like-minded individuals in your town or country. In recent years, the momentum of the CS discipline has increased massively and there are always eager professionals looking to get together so go out there and find them.

See also Glossary and Resources

Baseline
As part of the research phase of the DESIGN stage, you will have gathered the right data to understand your baseline position.

- How many customers do you have?
- What's the average account size?
- What's the current growth trend?
- How many support calls?
- How many users self-serve?
- What's your net/gross retention rate?
- What outcomes do you serve?
- Average time-to-value
- Length of onboarding process
- Number of training courses delivered
- Number of users trained
- Number of Business Reviews delivered
- And so on!

You will also, having designed your programme and framework on the customer journey and customer outcomes, have an idea of the impact you will expect to make, having implemented a proactive process.

- What customer outcomes do you want to serve?
- What's the target net/gross retention rate?
- Increase in and impact of training
- Reduction in time-to-value
- Number of referrals
- Account expansion plans
- And so on!

Benchmarking

Once you have established your baseline, you can use the aforementioned pilot approach to understand the impact you're making.

By making a simple change at a time, you can identify the impact that change is making and apply that benchmark to the rest of your portfolio and process.

While larger scale benchmarking can be sourced externally, it is hugely important to understand the impact of your own team, product, company culture, programme and objectives.

What we need to achieve and how we demonstrate the value will need to be tweaked to your own specific circumstances.

External benchmarking will be added into the mix and useful for further considerations and future development

- Domain and industry expertise and benchmarking

- o Customers WILL ask you 'What does good look like?' and you will need to understand that from a number of different angles, including industry perspectives (domain expertise) and also specifically for the use of your service
- Customer outcomes
  - o Customers rarely know how to articulate what they need and often don't know what their stated outcomes should be, so you have to help them get there
  - o They will ask 'What do my peers and competitors ask for?'
- Scaling Customer Success
  - o As you apply more frameworks and sign more customers, you will need to scale your processes and resources more effectively
  - o Options and techniques are improving constantly and this information is shared through articles, meet-ups and conferences
- Customer Success metrics and initiatives
  - o At the very least, your management are also going to ask, 'What does good look like?' so keep abreast of the trends within the discipline
  - o The discipline is being shaped as we work through our daily lives and learnings, keep up to date and contribute to the conversation and research

Benchmarking is largely about providing yourself with the information to conduct comparison and contrast analysis.

Who does what well? What do you do well and what could you be sharing with others? What are the enduring trends and techniques? How can we further improve our offering? How can I develop my team effectively?

Finding answers to all these questions and many more, gives you the power to aspire to be the very best in the field and support others to get there too:

- Attend conferences
- Arrange meet-ups
- Get involved in the local, country, continent and global communities
- Share your experiences and learnings
- Create a peer-to-peer network which provides value up and down the chain

Pioneer's round-up!

Key learnings

❖ You need to draw a line in the sand, before you start, to allow you to measure the progress you make and how far you've come

❖ Benchmarking information allows you to understand:
- ❑ How others have done it
- ❑ Where you are aiming
- ❑ Customer outcomes and expectations

❖ The Customer Success community is eager to share its experiences and knowledge; so use it!

❖ It is important to be able to define and articulate what good will look like for any implementation

Actions

❖ Document your baseline; draw your line in the sand

❖ Gather your benchmarking information and set your targets

❖ Define 'what good looks like' for this implementation phase

Hot tips

❖ Ensure you set time boundaries for when you will compare and contrast your expectations vs reality
- ❑ This will allow you to iterate in a timely and valuable manner

***

For more ideas and templates, download the companion workbook at www.thecspioneer.com/resources/workbook

Get in touch to share your thoughts, questions, challenges and triumphs: talk@thecspioneer.com

3.2 Customer Health

Customer Health is a small term for a wide subject.

What do we even mean by Customer Health and for what purpose are we using this information? Is it a metric, is it sentiment, is it science or an art-form?

There is a danger of getting too hung up on the idea of Customer Health and in particular the Customer Health Score (see below).

Moderation and balance are key. Start with a simple idea, ensure you're capturing the data and over time you'll understand which is the right data, for you and on which metrics to focus.

If you have a small portfolio, the chances are that you will know each customer intimately and taking the word of the accountable CSM will suffice, in the beginning. It is worth noting that it is NEVER too early to start collecting the evidence for what works.

What is Customer Health?

Customer Health, in the simplest of terms is a view of how healthy each customer account is, in terms of relationship, retention and growth.

In the research phase of the DESIGN stage, we talked about assigning a status to each customer; this is in effect, the Customer Health of each account.

It will be based on qualitative and quantitative data and gives an indication of how secure that account is. Will they renew, will they expand, will they provide referrals?

It will also be a key tool to manage your portfolio. We have already talked about segmenting your portfolio to help with the management of your customers, and Customer Health can help prioritise activity within these segments and by each CSM.

Whether you are making an instinctive decision about the status of a customer or you have built up a more sophisticated way to measure it, Customer Health is a key technique for understanding the overall health of your portfolio, where your champion customers are and also which accounts are 'at risk'.

You may hear Customer Health or at least the resulting trigger referred to as an Early Warning System (EWS), as any model which has been built or bought to monitor Customer Health will usually contain a trigger or alert to identify those accounts deemed to be at risk and requiring immediate attention and action.

What is a Customer Health Score?

A Customer Health Score, for some companies, is the key metric which outputs from any Customer Health model.

It may be expressed in whichever form you choose

- RAG (Red, Amber, Green) traffic light status report
- An absolute score (for example: X/100)
- A percentage
- Bespoke names relevant to your company

Whichever proxy is chosen for reporting, the imperative is to understand what the scale means. At which point, does a customer move from Green to Amber and Amber to Red? And vice versa? What does a score of 60 mean? Is it good, bad or indifferent; can a customer ever get to 100, for example?

The healthier the customer, the closer they are to being your ideal customer. As such, a low Customer Health Score doesn't necessarily mean a customer is going to churn. Instead, it tells the CSM that the customer needs help and support in order to strengthen their relationship with your company and gain more value from your solution.

Irit Eizips, CCO & CEO, CSM Practice

A Customer Health Score needs to be fully understood and this will only happen over time and if the algorithms underneath the single number, colour or name start in the simplest form, allowing validation of each qualitative and quantitative input.

The benefit of having a customer score is that it will become universally recognised within your company and if you choose to share it with your customers, externally too.

I would, usually, advocate for sharing the metric within your customer reporting. Your contract with them is a partnership with agreed responsibilities and undertakings on each side and as such, you should be able to tell them how the score will reflect the positive action you have each taken towards your joint goals.

Note: you will need to understand what the score indicates as the customer will definitely ask what it means and how they are doing against benchmarks or more specifically, your other customers who may well be their competitors!

Data to be included in the calculation of the health score can be quantitative (absolute) and qualitative (use of proxy) and certain inputs may be more heavily weighted than others, where appropriate

- Time-to-value achieved
- Onboarding and implementation experience
- Adoption and usage data
- Size of account
- Length of relationship to date
- Strength of relationship with key contacts
- Survey results
- Training undertaken
- Number of support calls
- Unresolved support calls
- Referral account?
- Growth and expansion of account
- Executive attendance at Business Reviews and events
- CSM judgement

As you can see the list of potential inputs is huge and there are plenty more not even listed here, so any attempt to create a Customer Health Score should be approached pragmatically, carefully and methodically.

In the early days, I started with the simplest of models and a RAG style status

- Red = At Risk; intervention required
- Amber = Work in Progress (WIP); proactive programming to continue and drive towards improvements
- Light Green = verbal agreement to renew or expand; engage with Sales/Renewal team to get the signature!
- Green = committed to renew

The inputs into this were length of contract, anecdotal evidence of our relationship to date and the latest view of the executive stakeholders at the customer; had the decision-maker made any indication they would renew?

We soon added in usage data, once we had cleaned it and ensured that only value-added actions were being included in 'Active User' status. We also applied a sliding scale of user statuses – login alone was not a convincing signal to renew!

Over time, we added in Support and Training data; however, the most important qualifier is the understanding the CSM gathers from their interactions with the customer. This is, naturally, harder with low-touch accounts, and metrics and targets will be adjusted accordingly depending on the segment.

Customer Health is a significant benefit to prioritising and managing your portfolio. However, we know that Customer Success is based on strong relationships so the human element must always be taken into consideration too.

Remember the warning tale of the Watermelon Customer – green on the outside but red on the inside. All the quantitative data was painting a green-filled picture, but had the qualitative data been taken into account or even collected?

There are ways to collect this data. The most preferred option is to get it straight from the horse's mouth – the Economic Buyer (EB). Whether you are able to get to the EB of every account or not, some companies use sentiment surveys, like the Net Promoter Score (or similar), to bridge this gap and to serve as a proxy.

As NPS is the most discussed, I've included a section below which digs into the process, pros and cons. The theories, concepts, benefits and warnings apply to the majority of surveys which you may choose to adopt.

Net Promoter Score (NPS)

The Net Promoter Score (NPS) is a measure which was formulated by Satmetrix and it is an index ranging from −100 to +100 that measures the willingness of customers to recommend a company's products or services to others. It is used as a proxy for gauging the customer's overall satisfaction with a company's product or service and the customer's loyalty to the brand.

NPS is very often used as a proxy for customer satisfaction and we have treated it as such in this book, to keep things simple.

It is therefore a tool which could be used as part of your customer satisfaction/Customer Health process.

An NPS survey is usually made up of one simple question:

> How likely is it that you would recommend our service/product to a friend or colleague?

The respondent then gets to choose a number between 0 and 10, depending on how they feel about you.

Noteworthy learnings:

It is always worth including an indication of one being less likely and ten being most likely

I once called a very loyal customer champion to as why they had given us a score of one. I couldn't imagine what we had done to annoy them so badly! They assured me that they had given me the highest score as they assumed that one was the top mark. Are aces high or low? That's a debate most amateur card players have each time they play. Seasoned hands state the scale definition right at the beginning, before play commences.

Consider the order of the scale

Some people believe that ten should be on the left as we read left to right and we have a very short attention span so we'll click on the first number we see. Others believe that we are trained to expect the higher value of the scale on the far right and will therefore click on that part of the scale without really registering any of the numbers! Which do you think is more likely?

Consider the sample size and feasible poll frequency

This is easier if you're sending out the NPS for a focal reason e.g. a new product release or a conference you delivered. Some companies poll their customers on a periodic basis through the year and it is worth contemplating the overall size of the candidate pool and also on what basis you will include your customers

- Totally random regardless of length of tenure or time of year signed
- Select customers on the anniversary of the contract date
- Include users n months after they have been created/trained

While some importance is attached to the NPS score achieved at any given polling, it is much more important to pay attention to the trend. Is it going up (Good) or down (Bad)?

How to calculate your NPS

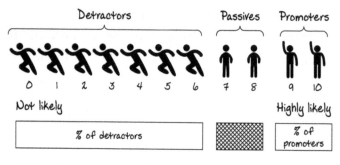

NPS = % of promoters - % of detractors

Figure 3.1: Net Promoter Score question and calculation

Calculation steps

Step 1: Find the total number of detractor and promoter responses

NB: Ignore all Passive responses

Step 2: Sum the number of detractors and convert to a percentage using the total identified in the first step

Step 3: Repeat for the promoters

Step 4: Subtract % of Detractors from % of Promoters and that's your NPS

Worked example

	Example 1	Example 2	Example 3	Example 4
Promoters	–	20	60	6
Passives	~~120~~	~~50~~	~~25~~	~~75~~
Detractors	6	23	10	–
Total Responses	**6**	**43**	**70**	**6**
% Promoters	0%	47%	86%	100%
% Detractors	100%	53%	14%	0%
NPS	**-100**	**-7**	**71**	**100**

Figure 3.2: NPS Worked example

Follow-up

You might be pleased as punch if your NPS is positive, such as in example 3 or 4, but what happens over time, if you leave the respondents to stagnate without any interaction?

One of the reasons the passives are ignored is because of a belief that they are not committed supporters and therefore could be turned either way. As evidenced by my reluctance to dish out 9s and 10s even to companies of which I'm quite fond, someone would need to be a passionate advocate to be a true promoter.

This means they will shout from the rooftops about you and your product, they will advocate for you, they will become and are your extended sales team.

Passives, therefore, can be quietly dangerous. They quite like you and your product but wouldn't fight to keep you. What would it take for them to slip from an eight to a seven and then to a six or lower. One conversation with a colleague who is already grumbling and complaining about you?

Detractors, by their very name, are devaluing your product and service every time they open their mouth or type a message to someone, on the subject of your company's offering. It only takes one dissenting voice to make a shaky renewal fall through and how many passives will be tempted over to the dark side by a single conversation by the water cooler (old school!) with one of their detractor colleagues?

Without any action from your team and company, NPS is a means to highlight to individuals how they feel about your product. Your customers will be aware of the surveys being sent to their teams, they may ask for the results and they will definitely ask their staff what they think of your product. What if they ask one of the many passives out there, feeling a little lukewarm about you?

Follow-up then, is key. Ensure that you factor this into your process and resourcing needs when defining how you will implement any survey. Once initiated, be very sure that follow-up is happening after *every* survey instance. Ensure the habit is created from the get-go and maintained religiously.

Follow-up actions

From the highest priority, these are some of the areas to consider and reasons why you should ensure follow-up is an integral part of any survey process.

Detractors: these need to be neutralised, at the very least. And fast. Simply, the fewer detractors you have, the stronger your extended sales team will be and you will have minimised the opportunities for them to persuade passives and even promoters that their negative viewpoint is the one true view. In many cases, a simple call will neutralise this threat. We're all individuals, we just want to be heard and in this day and age where the personal touch is so often overthrown for automation, we are disarmed by an organisation reaching out to us to let us know we've been heard.

Identify why they don't love it and take an action to make it better or explain to them how they can use it to better advantage.

Were they onboarded properly? Get them remedial onboarding and fix the gap in your process which allowed this to happen in the first place.

Do they need advanced training to show them new features and expert methods for achieving their objectives? Book them some time with a trainer or onto the next webinar and make your training offerings more accessible. Talk to the product team to get some/more in-app signposting and support.

Passives: these are excluded from the NPS calculation as it is thought they are sitting on the fence – neither promoters nor

184 | Design. Implement. Measure. Evolve (DIME)

detractors ("see note below). The threat here is that they could topple off the fence into the shady area of detractors. Wouldn't it be better for them to be encouraged into the green pastures of the promoters where they will become your cheerleaders and a solid part of your virtual sales team?

As with the detractors, a simple call could suffice. For larger scale operations, some well thought out and designed automated communications could work just as well. Understand the underlying causes of the feedback, get to the root of any discontent or indifference and highlight an attractive path to the right side.

Promoters: these form your virtual sales army. You want to make sure they work as hard as possible on your behalf.

As with most actions, timing is important. However, we are all usually resource constrained so I would thoroughly recommend that you concentrate on the detractors and then the passives, in order to neutralise those threats. You know what they say about it only taking one bad apple to spoil the whole barrel.

Another thing to consider, always and with any part of your Customer Success programming, is that this is a company-wide responsibility. You may own what and how things need to be done but it's the responsibility of the whole company to deliver on this framework.

Promoters should be thanked, positive feedback gathered and a request made to become a published advocate for you – permission given for a case study, an official reference account

---

* Note: In the UK, we're pretty reserved so if I *love* something and I mean *really love it*, I'm likely to give you an 8.

to be used in the sales cycle and on your website as a clear indication of the value your product gives recognised and high-worth brands.

The gathering of references and case studies is often the role of a Marketing department so make it their responsibility, when you draw up your full programming, to manage this area of the survey process. For some companies, there is a Customer Marketing team and they might manage the whole survey process while it still forms part of your overall Customer Success programming. This is a great example of Customer Success being truly cross-functional and it is therefore imperative that teams all work together with a truly customer-aligned focus.

Pioneer's round–up!

Key learnings

❖ Customer Health is the measurement activity utilised to predict the status of a customer in relation to their likelihood to renew, grow and make referrals

❖ A Customer Health Score (CHS) is a metric created to provide a recognisable proxy from which to prioritise and develop your portfolio focus and activities

❖ NPS is most often used as a proxy for qualitative customer satisfaction (Cust Sat)

   ❑ This requires company-wide commitment to acting on the feedback provided by the customer

   ❑ The process can be an excellent way to gather critical opinions on how to improve your product and processes

   ❑ You must acknowledge and follow up with your customers

Actions

❖ Create, understand and communicate your Customer Health approach and proxy

❖ Ensure you learn your lessons from all your customer accounts

   ❑ What did you do well?

   ❑ What needs improving?

   ❑ Pay particular attention to reasons for churn, especially if you thought the account was 'safe'

   ❑ Monitor your approach and incorporate lessons learned and feedback from any surveys issued

Hot tips

❖ Design an approach which is simple to create, prove and understand; it is possible to evolve over time so don't fall into the trap of over-complicating from the start

❖ Beware the 'watermelon effect' (green on the outside, red on the inside); learn lessons and effect change from these customers

❖ The departure of a customer champion can be an opportunity as well as a risk
  ❑ The departing champion may take you with them to their new company

❖ If you convert detractors, they can become your fiercest allies and promoters!

**

For more ideas and templates, download the companion workbook at www.thecspioneer.com/resources/workbook

Get in touch to share your thoughts, questions, challenges and triumphs: talk@thecspioneer.com

3.3 Demonstrating Value

> *It is my belief that, when done right, Customer*
> *Success needs little justification at all*
>
> Maria Martinez, former President, Sales and
> Customer Success at Salesforce

This quotation was once the opening slide of a presentation I delivered on the subject of demonstrating value to the C-Suite and the company.

I asked for a vote from the conference delegates as to whether they agreed with this sentiment and got about a 50% split.

I can understand this. I agree with Maria – when done right, it needs little justification. There is a lot of depth behind this quotation, which was included in the foreword of Gainsight's Customer Success book: *Customer Success: How Innovative Companies are Reducing Churn and Growing Recurring Revenue.*

The reasoning is based upon the basic premise for the existence of Customer Success.

See also Part I: Customer Success is...?

Maria continues, in her foreword, to explain her view of this:
- It preserves the company's book of business, opens doors for additional opportunities and creates lifelong advocates in our customers

- When optimised, Customer Success is the best sales and marketing engine possible
- Customer Success is more than just the right thing to do, it is a business imperative
- The Customer Success team is held accountable for customer usage, adoption and ultimately revenue
- *Our success is directly tied to that of our customers*

This last point ties into my assertion that Customer Success = Company Success (Their Success = Our Success)

If all the pieces of your Customer Success programme are in the right place and all the people are playing their parts to the best of their ability, then the need for justification should be very light.

The inherent value would be understood and validated by the uplift in retention rates (both gross and net), the increase in sales and referrals and any NPS or customer satisfaction frameworks which are in place. The C-Suite, investors and people signing the cheques would understand the value Customer Success is bringing to the company not only through these revenue metrics but because Customer Success is the heartbeat of the company. Customer focus is how the organisation breathes and succeeds.

Why then, the need to demonstrate value?

There are many factors to explain why the need to demonstrate value is constantly weighing heavy in most organisations:

Customer Success is still relatively new as a distinct discipline and many companies are still unaware of it. In circumstances where they are aware of it, many are paying lip service to it because they need to keep their investors (VCs) happy. Some think it's a trend, which will pass, so why invest serious money, time and energy into it?

An additional challenge with the discipline still being nascent is that no one really knows a failsafe approach to establishing and propagating a successful team. When you think about it, we're all making it up as we go along. That's what pioneering is, that's what innovation and evolution are. You have to have faith that you are doing the right things to get you where you need to be.

Consider then, that a management team might have to decide between 'throwing good money after bad' (i.e. Customer Success in their mind) and 'investing in the established field of Sales' – for them, it seems like an easy decision.

This brings me to the next factor. Investment. While VCs are driving the conversation around the inherent value in Customer Success in the age of the subscription economy and SaaS, the C-Suite and in particular, the Finance Director (Chief Financial Officer/CFO) may need a little more persuading. In larger, enterprise companies which are transitioning to SaaS and still have a healthy chunk of legacy on-premise business in their portfolio, this can be even more of a challenge to justify as they are much more slow-moving and unwieldy vessels like the oil tankers, traversing the oceans at a snail's pace.

In times of cashflow challenges, only those departments which can be directly connected to revenue *generating* activities will be given priority.

Revenue *generating* is the key perspective here too. Customer Success is all about revenue – retaining and growing. It's also a far more efficient and cost-effective approach to growing your revenue. It is, however, much harder to identify exactly *how* Customer Success has made an impact beyond the 'touchy, feely' and hand-holding that is associated with the department by most executives who have yet to embrace the age of the customer as a revenue growth engine.

Very few Customer Success teams, particularly in EMEA although it is more common in the US, have a selling price attached to their services. Customers expect the partnership to come as part of the 'service' for which they are paying. I understand this and subscribe to this philosophy, as a general rule, from the customer perspective. Build the cost of the team and activities into the Service cost. You are, after all, selling your product as a service, so include the Service element!

Internally, however, you need to itemise and promote the contributions made by each area of the business. If the cost of the service hasn't been broken down into its component parts, I would suggest that's a great place to start to show your value and worth.

Why it's worth your time and investment

There are plenty of modern-day stories (and they are not fairy tales) about companies taking the decision to axe their entire Customer Success teams (e.g. Zendesk and Microsoft) only to then reinstate the concept and then travel full circle a number of times. This will, no doubt, be a valuable learning exercise each time it occurs. However, it is painful for the business and for all the individuals involved. It is unnecessary stress for all, costs the business more in the long run and ultimately is due to a lack of data and demonstrable value.

While I have not experienced such a brutal outcome, I did make the mistake of assuming that everyone knew and understood the value my team and I were bringing to the table.

A valuable lesson: it never hurts and always helps to have data which validates your existence!

Data is without doubt your greatest friend and ally when you are considering how to run your team, your customer portfolio and your priorities. Due to my IT, Finance and Project background, I knew with absolute clarity that data needed to be surfaced and understood to create a valuable and successful programme.

I absolutely understood that my internal partners needed to understand the customer data to buy in to the programme. My mistake was underestimating how important it was to demonstrate clear value in absolute terms to my fellow leadership team members.

I thought they were in it with me. And they were, to a point.

I could have and should have accessed better investment and understanding across the board if I had ensured I demonstrated our value (which was even higher than they already assumed they knew), consistently and frequently.

Arguments for Customer Success value

- The cost of new sales is significantly higher than the cost of retaining customers
  - Ensure continued focus on and investment in Customer Success
- We are no longer in the captive audience world of on-premise hardware and maintenance contracts
  - Customers have choices, it is easier for them to swap supplies or stop using a service altogether
- Power has shifted from vendor to customer
  - We need to ensure we work with customers to ensure continued partnerships
- Maximise the ability and capability to minimise churn and sustain real growth
- Customer Success is a philosophy and it must pervade the whole company
  - Customer Success requires a top-down, company-wide commitment to truly deliver world-class Customer Success

Foundations may have been shaky from the start; did you, your predecessor, your SLT or anyone do strong groundwork to ensure everyone understood and was committed to customer focus and Customer Success as an embedded philosophy?

Did the CEO change since the commitment was made or other key influencers in the organisation? Were they talked through the philosophy, did they challenge it, did they embrace it? Revisit the foundations activities, if needed.

See also 1.2 Foundations and Beliefs

To whom do we need to demonstrate value?

The C-Suite and the company: surely, they are one and the same?

Earlier, I referred to a presentation I delivered discussing the need to demonstrate value to the C-Suite and your company. As with the highlighted quotation from Maria Martinez, I asked for a vote from the room on whether these were two different requirements or the same set of recipients with the same requirements, needs and sentiments.

Again, the room was split.

I can understand why some would believe the C-Suite would need and want the same information as the rest of the company. And vice versa. I would counter that they are different sets of stakeholders, have different expectations of and from you. Equally, the value you demonstrate to each of them will be nuanced by your needs and requirements from each of them.

Therefore, I argue for the need to understand the different cohorts and stakeholders to whom you need to demonstrate value, and adjust the information you provide accordingly. There will, naturally, be some crossover. Some of the C-Suite information will be desirable for the company to know and equally, some of the company information will be of interest to the C-Suite. Conversely, the C-Suite is likely to want much higher-level headlines, metrics and KPIs rather than getting all the details on which some other decisions must be based.

The C-Suite, for example, will not need to know all the level of detail that the Product Development team will need from you in order to get them to prioritise an important customer's feature request or bug fix.

For this reason, I will handle the stakeholder subsets separately below when we discuss to whom we need to demonstrate value and how we might approach this.

- C-Suite
- Company
- Customers
- Other stakeholders (e.g. investors, prospects)
- Prospects

How we demonstrate value

To truly demonstrate value, we need to review the data we've been collecting, the benchmarks that we have researched and the impacts we've measured as a result of our proactive programme implementations.

 In Sales, a key performance indicator (KPI) is the Cost of Acquiring a Customer (CAC); this metric exists to ensure a company wins profitable business, i.e. that there is an acceptable margin between revenue and the costs associated with winning that income. Costs would likely include Account Manager costs, sales operations costs, technology, events, marketing costs, etc.

In addition to this, there needs to be proof that the contract is profitable while in operation. Costs to be applied here would include support costs, any reactive help from the Customer Success team and any apportioned cost of events. There is also an argument for considering the spreading of engineering and product costs for the specific product that customers have. This is typically called Cost to Serve (CTS).

A retention metric has appeared into the mix and this is the Cost of Retaining a Customer (CRC).

This helps to answer the question around whether growth is sustainable or profitable. At this point, we need to include the cost of resources dedicated to retaining and growing your existing accounts. This number needs to be lower than the revenue associated with existing accounts (renewals and expansion).

Use these metrics together to understand Sales, Retention and Growth

Profit of original contract = Contract Revenue – CAC – CTS

Profit of renewing contract = total new revenue (including renewal and growth) – CTS – CRC

Typically, because of scale, relationships and the value of Customer Success, CRC is far lower than CAC in most accounts. This proves that Customer Success drives more profitable contracts once they have landed.

Where you find this not to be the case, investigation needs to be undertaken in terms of the programme content, the commitment to deliver on responsibilities by both yourselves and the customer and any other variable elements which may be counter-productive or candidates for streamlining.

 A more straightforward way to implement this, particularly to begin with, is to calculate the average cost of retaining a customer by dividing the annualised customer retention costs by the total number of active customers. If you want the average CRC for the customer's lifetime multiply CRC by the average customer lifetime.

Some of the other headline metrics we discussed in earlier chapters will also show instant value as you show an upward trend

- Gross Retention Rate
  - o Need to be aiming for at least 95% gross retention for any period
- Net Retention Rate
  - o Target an exceptional net retention rate of at least 125% for any period
  - o If you target growing companies for all new business, there will come a time when you could rely on your existing portfolio to continue a stellar growth rate, without then ever contracting a single piece of additional new business

Are these headline metrics enough? Will they motivate the teams and customers who need to commit to deliver on their responsibilities?

C-Suite

While you're getting to the proof positive using the CRC, CAC and CTS and even beyond this time, there will be additional motivations that the C-Suite will require.

Based on experience, here are some recommendations for how to work with the C-Suite or level of Senior Management into whom you report.

- Agree Objectives of Customer Success function
  - Reduce/manage churn
  - Increased contract value for installed base
  - Improve customer experience and customer satisfaction
- Agree Key Metrics which are measurable and trackable
  - Retention (Gross and/or Net)
  - Targets for Metrics (i.e. 120% Retention)
  - References/case studies
  - Bring Your Own App ('second-order revenue')
  - Referrals
  - NPS or similar
  - Customer Lifetime Value (LTV)
- Identify Opportunity costs/profit/loss
- Report, analyse and discuss agreed metrics
  - Include usage statistics, at high level
  - Highlight priorities using exception reporting

The company

The company at large will still be interested in the headline statistics which you've agreed with the C-Suite; however they have their own day jobs and responsibilities on which to focus.

They will congratulate you when you announce an improvement and a consistent positive trend. They will congratulate themselves, as you will remind them that this journey is one in which you're all together, working hard and achieving results, delivering joint objectives and responsibilities.

However, day to day, they will be drawn back to the minutiae of their own jobs and may perhaps lose the customer focus which they've promised to embrace.

Here are some of the approaches to adopt to promote that laser focus on Customer Success

- Continual promotion of the customer-centric culture
- Communicate agreed objectives of Customer Success
- Report achievements
  - Dashboards
  - Company newsletters
- Identify relevance for each function within the organisation
- Communicate the impact for each function
- Maintain partnerships with each function
- Highlight impact of misalignment
  - Customer failure
  - Higher Support calls
  - Fewer sales; minimal company advancement
- Usage statistics
  - For customer
  - For internal recognition and impact of achievements
  - For C-Suite
  - Caveat: usage statistics are a great indicator of adoption within a customer base, however they don't prove that the decision-makers see the value in your product so be wary of relying solely on these
- Shout-outs at key company events to individuals/functions contributing most widely to CS achievements in that period

- Share customers' vision to consolidate partnership from each corner of the business

In fairness, there is some overlap between these first two stakeholder groups, particularly as the C-Suite are *part* of the company so all of the points here are relevant to them as being part of this group of people.

Customers and prospects

Each of the stakeholder groups we've highlighted here are crucial to success in your mission, and the customer is perhaps 'more equal than the others' as you have to be successful in retaining and growing your customers to have a great story to tell the company and your C-Suite.

Identify how your customers measure success, and get their buy-in to provide data from their systems and processes to prove the impact your partnership is having on their business. Understand what is important to the Economic Buyer and the customer programme manager and align yourself to their goals.

In this way, you can demonstrate the value of your partnership and your role as trusted advisor, in addition to the value of your product through the measurement of their KPIs and RoI for your contract.

Being able to demonstrate their position relative to their peers and competitors will also be important here, so the benchmarking and baseline activity we discussed will really come into its own here.

The capture of the business objectives should be first undertaken during the prospecting stage of your relationship with potential customers and updated regularly as you proceed along the journey with them as contracted customers.

Prospects will also be highly interested in the benchmark data you have gathered and the results your established customers are reporting. This helps your product sell itself by demonstrating the inherent value of implementing, retaining and expanding the use of it.

Final word on the approach to demonstrating value

This approach has proven effective for a number of companies from whom I've heard their experiences in this area.

Cisco, for example, ran a pilot scheme where a number of customers were given a CSM and a programme. Data was collected on these customers and analysed to understand the impact of them having the benefit of a CSM vs customers who remained on the legacy way of running the portfolio, i.e. left to their own devices.

The results were overwhelmingly positive and there's no refuting the proof of data, so the Customer Success programme was embraced and embedded in the company culture. They even run their own Customer Success Certification programme, which is open to delegates who are not employees.

This is a great way to prove the value of your Customer Success offering. It may be easier to approach the issue in this way in a traditional enterprise company who are transitioning to SaaS or merely embracing the customer focus which Customer Success inherently brings to a company. The company has a portfolio of customers languishing without any love or guidance so it's easy to pick a few customers for whom to trial the new approach, track and report back to the senior leadership team.

NB: It would be recommended to ensure the pilot customers cover a range of good customers, at risk, average, etc.

This will also work in a smaller organisation, as long as you ensure you have understood the baseline and can assess the impact of having a reactive only approach (by using a control group) to managing your customers.

However, there are always customers who are unresponsive – they are almost always the customers which churn. Consider ways to reach them and demonstrate the value here.

Pioneer's round-up!

Key learnings

❖ Done right, Customer Success needs little justification
  ❑ HOWEVER, we are still in a period of enlightenment and education so it should be a high priority of any CS leader to continually and effectively demonstrate value
❖ Taking the time to show value will prove worthwhile
  ❑ To bring you the required investment to grow and develop your programme and time
  ❑ To save your team from being dismissed as 'nice to have' and 'cost-draining'
  ❑ To enlighten your company as to the imperative of embedding Customer Success and to show them how you contribute to their continuing existence
❖ Value needs to be demonstrated, as motivation for commitment and investment of time and money, to everyone
  ❑ Your colleagues; to ensure they will support your programme and undertake their customer-focused activities
  ❑ The C-Suite and Investors; to obtain the required investment into your team and programme
  ❑ Stakeholders and partners; to give them the motivation to support and promote you
  ❑ Your customers; so they understand the value they are getting from you in terms of having a Trusted Advisor and getting RoI
  ❑ Prospects; so they will want to join you on your journey

❖ Agreed objectives, metrics, priorities and reporting will help align the C-Suite to your cause and smooth the activities of demonstrating value

Actions

❖ Attach value to each of your activities, to demonstrate your inherent worth to Investors and the C-Suite
❖ Create and use a schedule of key metrics to demonstrate your value
  ❑ Religiously update and refine
  ❑ Effectively and regularly promote the story these metrics tell
❖ Understand the CRC and CAC at your company; this should provide a powerful way to show value
  ❑ The CRC should be significantly lower than the CAC; investigate and adapt your programme and activities, if this is not the case

Hot tips

❖ Running a pilot (or having a control group) can be an impactful way of demonstrating the impact and value of Customer Success

***

For more ideas and templates, download the companion workbook at www.thecspioneer.com/resources/ workbook

Get in touch to share your thoughts, questions, challenges and triumphs: talk@thecspioneer.com

4.0 DIME cycle stage: Evolve

Adapting your map to maximise the impact of your journey to growth

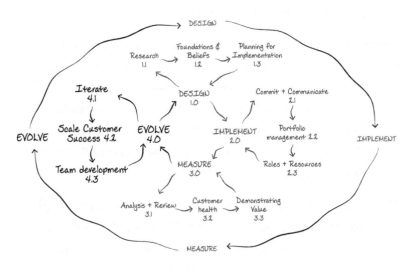

4.1 Iterate

Customer Success is a partnership with a long-term focus rather than a service with set and short-term deliverables.

It's about helping your customer get the value they need from your product to help them achieve their business outcomes. Some would say that you need to achieve this quickly and it's true that the shorter the time-to-value, the more likely it is that customers will buy into your programme and stay with you for a little longer.

However, what you really want to get them to understand (quickly) is that you are there for the long haul. You have their best interests at heart and you are going to work with them, in an aligned and committed partnership.

There is a lot of operational focus to get this philosophy embedded and the customer experience seamless. It needs a team that owns it and is accountable for its achievement. This team is Customer Success and without this committed co-ordination, customers are unlikely to achieve their outcomes, see value in your product or renew their contract, let alone expand or refer you to their network.

Through the preparation, design, implementation, measurement and evolution of your Customer Success journey, this is the objective towards which you travel. There is no final destination as partnerships evolve and iterate into more challenging, ambitious and rewarding dynamics.

Part of your evolution will be to iterate and improve exponentially each time.

You will achieve this through continual feedback, analysis and adjustment to all the elements (and more) which we've discussed within this book

- Mission
- Vision
- Business Outcomes
- Revenue Targets
- Customer Journey map
- Customer Experience
- Customer Satisfaction
- Sustainability
- Programme
- Processes
- Automation
- Portfolio management
- CSM technology
- Reporting lines
- Compensation plans

If you've adopted a pilot approach or perhaps an agile environment, you will be ensuring this happens as a matter of operational imperative.

It is healthy for any business to review its operations on a periodic and regular basis and this is even more crucial while we are pioneering Customer Success in the relatively new world of the subscription economy and as even more transformational change is predicted.

James Russell, at Bazaarvoice, highlighted the importance of the iterative approach they have been employing there, for their long tail portfolio over the last few years, to strengthen the strategy and impact they were having to achieve their customer outcomes and their business goals.

At each iteration, they have provided a structure and then monitored and listened to feedback from customers and employees.

James ensures they understand the pain points, as well as the activities they are doing well and do something about them to enable and empower their resources. They are learning from each iteration and getting stronger and more effective and efficient at each round.

It is imperative to review your programme regularly:

- When your portfolio goes through substantial growth
- When your company is at its different stages of maturity
- When or if business priorities change
- As you learn from significant customer feedback/wins/ losses

Adapt for success and business priorities

The MEASURE and EVOLVE stages, as with all stages in the cycle, are intrinsically linked to each other as the observations and analysis undertaken in the MEASURE stage will form the basis for understanding any adjustments which will be required to the programme you have started to implement.

In the early days of implementing any change, particularly a business shift in philosophy as we've discussed, it is crucial to keep a close eye on the results of your actions to understand how they align to your intentions.

We are looking to form lasting relationships with our clients to bring them value to their long-term business outcomes and goals. We need to make sure we cement this view solidly, effectively and in a timely manner.

Therefore, we should be on a continual review approach. If you've been running a series of pilots to implement the bigger programme, you'll be working towards adapting your activities during each release.

These are some of the questions that you may want to address, while considering your iteration approach:

- What did we do well?
- What could we have done better?
- How can we learn and improve moving forwards?
- Have we listened to and delivered for our customers?
- Did it work?
  - Did our retention rate improve?
  - Were our customers more satisfied?
  - Are Customers at the heart of everything we do?
  - Have we truly understood that Customer Success is our path to sustainable and exceptional growth?
  - Have we moved as expected towards our defined objectives?
    - Do we need to adjust our objectives?

- Are the activities being undertaken as planned? Are they having the desired results? Are they the most effective they can be?
- Are they aligned to our customers' and our own business priorities?

Review business priorities and customer outcomes

Many of the elements of your programme will be affected by the business priorities and outcomes identified by your customers and your own company.

This isn't to say that you should adapt your programme indiscriminately each time you hear a piece of news which is different to your current understanding and way of working.

However, you should give each piece of information careful consideration and credence. Take the time to understand how it fits into your philosophy and programme education and delivery.

Do they work well together? If there is a gap, does it need adjusting? Does your way of working positively impact the way a customer thinks they should be working?

For this last point, remember that we are looking to establish long-term partnerships and to be regarded as trusted advisors. If you believe that something you're doing will benefit the customer, talk to them about adapting to you rather than contorting yourself to their ideas. We're in this together!

Reasons for churn/reasons for renewing or expanding

An activity, for which many people don't find the time, is to identify those customers who have cancelled during the period under review.

Of course, I hear you cry, we would be painfully aware of customers who had churned. You're more than likely being measured on this and incentivised to reduce this occurrence!

Do you take the next step and identify *WHY* they made this decision to leave you?

Sometimes, it can be hard to hear criticism but we need to embrace constructive feedback and ensure we limit these cases in the future.

Occasionally, there will be nothing you could have done. All the signs will have been positive, all the joint responsibilities achieved and still the Economic Buyer had no choice but to say no to a renewal.

But.

There will be plenty of opportunities to improve.

Is it a particular product or product feature? Is it a lengthy and unwieldy process? Is it a lack of stickiness or adoption? Are you missing something really simple from your messaging, processes or product?

 Similarly, look at your customers who are renewing and even more so, those who are growing their commitment to you. What are you getting right for them?

We know that case studies are great for referrals and as part of a virtual sales process but do you take the time to review the details of the case study to understand the top reasons that customer is such a fan? Perhaps you did something, at a pivotal moment, which had a magnifying ripple effect and you could embed this into your process as a sustainable win.

Unpack and explore the reasons for each of these cases and use this information to adapt your programme accordingly. Is your support process seamless and frictionless to allow easy resolution of queries and product issues? How is your onboarding delighting customers and how can you incorporate this into other processes?

Fill any gaps you uncover in your customers' reasons for churn and do more of the great stuff that not only keeps your customers but leads them to grow their own commitment to you and provide new customers for you too.

 Prioritise and do more of the good stuff and minimise the activities which distract you, provide less value and contribute to churn!

Selling to the right customer

One of the things you should start doing more of, if you're not already committed to this, is ensure that the entire company is selling to the right customer.

Put another way, one thing you should stop doing immediately is selling to the wrong customer.

For some sales teams, any customer is the right customer. In the legacy world of transactions, this may well have had an element of truth to it. Get them in the door and then move onto the next sale. Obviously, I would propose that this should never be the case, in history and definitely not today.

Knowing the profile of your ideal customer is crucial to providing value. If you sell to customers you cannot help, you will be doing them a disservice and you'll also be setting yourselves up for a fall.

As we've seen with NPS, stellar experiences are often shouted about but so are those where we feel we've been cheated in some way.

 Use the EVOLVE stage to understand your customers better and work with your Sales team to understand the right customer profile.

If you are honest and upfront with your customers, your reputation will exponentially improve and word will spread.

You can even refer the 'wrong-fit' customers to companies which *are* able to help them. In the future, should these customers become the right fit, they will come to you before anyone else because of your willingness to do the right thing.

You can define the profile in a more detailed way by using the analysis of the activity above:

- For which reasons do customers churn?
- Why do customers stay?
- Why do customers expand their commitment with us?
- For which stated reasons do customers refer us to others in their network?
- What do we do well and should do more of?
- What can we improve and how?
- What should we stop doing?

Product impact

The Product team should be one of your most closely aligned internal partnerships. A great product, with stickiness and responsiveness to customer feedback, is a key feature of a company which cares about its customers and their needs.

The EVOLVE stage will likely include significant feedback to the Product team although this will also form part of your operational process. It is important to find a way to communicate customer needs and comments to the Product team with enough notice to be accommodated into the product release cycle.

This may result in customer-facing features and functionality or perhaps some in-app capability for internal teams to ensure that processes are as efficient and frictionless as possible. Each little tweak will help you get to the best value you can offer to maximise the impact of Customer Success on your customers' outcomes and your growth ambitions.

An important perspective to have when reviewing your programme and the product is how to embed yourself in your customers' processes. How do you become so sticky that you're irreplaceable or, at the least, it would take immense efforts to consider replacing you?

The Product team will also use this opportunity to talk to you about their needs from you in the process and to get your support in getting specific information from customers in relation to the roadmap.

In some circumstances, the Product team may require your assistance in finding beta testers for a particular feature or functionality. This may be a key component of a Customer Advisory Board (CAB) if you have created something like this for your customer programme.

Communication

No matter how long you've been in the business world, you will be aware how important communication is to achieve anyone's goals.

Without clear, concise and timely communication, teams will be working in silos, with customers unaware of product improvements or objectives reached.

Communication is also two-way: we talked so far about gathering and assessing information to support your next evolution. This is communicating for the purposes of receiving information from others.

It is equally important to ensure you communicate outwards and back to those who need to be informed of the changes and the value already achieved

- Product team; two-way communication on product topics and in-app tools

- Internal teams; updates to processes
- Company; demonstrating value, highlighting gaps and identifying resolutions through the next iteration
- Programme content; ensure this is updated at each iteration to align with changes you make as well as product release updates
- Customer feedback; where specific issues were raised, ensure you loop back and update the affected customers
- Customer updates; keep the customer updated in a timely manner for changes to process, programme and product
- Business Reviews; demonstrate value through the MEASURE activities and trust through those from the EVOLVE stage. Prove that you are listening to them and acting upon what you are hearing from them

Frequency and channel of communication needs a balance and will likely differ from company to company based on business priorities and types of customer. As with the overall customer programme and philosophy, you will need to monitor this periodically to assess the impact and whether any changes need to be made.

Pioneer's round-up!

Key learnings

❖ Long-term partnerships require continual feedback, assessment and adjustment

❑ The activity of continual development and evolution must be given and remain a priority

❖ The reasons why customers churn will provide essential insight into how you need to develop and evolve your programme and objectives further

❑ Learn from these customers to minimise the future impact of churn

❖ The EVOLVE stage will provide valuable content and context for your ideal customer profile

❑ Getting the profile correctly defined will help you avoid potentially damaging customer experiences

❑ Sticking to the correctly defined profile when courting prospects will allow you to enhance your reputation as a trusted advisor committed to doing the right thing for your customers

Actions

❖ Dedicate solid time to undertaking and fully understanding the feedback, analysis and iteration process

❖ Understand the reasons why customers churn and TAKE ACTION

❖ Identify the most value-add and sustainable activities which keep your customers loyal and committed

❑ Do more of this!

❖ Use the Iterate phase to feedback your findings to support the Product roadmap, in terms of the customer experience and perspective

Hot tips

❖ Always review your success as well as those customers which churn
  ❑ There will be effective and sustainable lessons to be learned which can achieve an enhancing ripple impact

***

For more ideas and templates, download the companion workbook at www.thecspioneer.com/resources/workbook

Get in touch to share your thoughts, questions, challenges and triumphs: talk@thecspioneer.com

4.2 Scale Customer Success

For some of you, you'll already be at the stage where you want to know how to scale your operations. Your portfolio and processes are already too resource heavy and you want to be able to implement efficiencies and automation to make your reach wider and deeper, for the investment you have available to you.

For others, it may be that the Adapt phase we've just talked about may last some time, maybe even years if your 'right-fit' customer is large enterprise companies and you have a very boutique-sized portfolio which absolutely requires high-touch, one-to-one engagement.

At some point, your company is likely to want to scale operations, perhaps move into a new sector or geography. Chances are, you'll want to find a scalable process as early as possible to maximise the value-add time you and your team are able to spend with each customer.

What does scalable mean?

 Scalability describes the ability of a process or organisation to grow and manage increased demand, in a sustainable manner.

This is specifically important to Customer Success because we see the discipline as being the function which builds long-term relationships to deliver value towards customers achieving their business outcomes.

Relationships with individuals – an objective which is, generally, expected to take the form of human interactions. How else would you build trusted, valuable and sustainable partnerships?

There are a few concepts to consider here

- Engagement models based on portfolio size and segments
- Process synergies
- Empower and enable CSMs

Engagement model

The chances are, whether you've formalised it or not, the first engagement model employed is that of high-touch.

All customers are treated equally, in the early days of applying high-touch by default. Customers may be large or small at this stage but each one is a keeper and there might not be time or capacity to consider that while all customers are important, it may be possible to differentiate the way they are handled and prioritised.

There may also be a tendency to concentrate on the larger customers, and there is danger here for a few reasons:

- Did you accurately identify the 'larger' or 'important' customers?
- How important is the retention rate to your company, including logo retention?
- Smaller or quieter customers can often be neglected to the detriment of revenue and/or reputation in the short and long term
  - It only takes one detractor to ripple far and wide to make a big impact on the future of your portfolio and potential growth

o   Remember the saying; 'one bad apple spoils the cart'?

This is going to hurt as a long-term strategy. Remember, we highlighted the need to make the time to stand back and assess your processes. This includes how to manage your customers and portfolio segments.

See also 2.2 Portfolio management

The segments that you define will likely be mapped onto the engagement models described here and you will need a strategy for how to deal with each segment to allow you to scale efficiently and successfully.

Each of these engagement models do what they say on the tin.

High-touch

A high-touch engagement model will likely be applied to customers who fit one or more of the following criteria

- High value contract
- Potential future high value contract
- Low value but high impact/profile brand or logo
  o   Particularly if the customer prefers high-touch interaction
- Early adopters with high referral rates and roadmap involvement

High-touch usually involves

- Dedicated CSM for the account
- CSMs have few accounts to manage
- Regular contact with various levels of stakeholders at the customer

- Quarterly Business Review with executive level attendance, including Economic Buyer
- Tailored Customer Success plan
- Full product functionality explored and exploited
- Trusted Advisor consulting approach
- All channels open
  - Monthly F2F meetings
  - In-person quarterly reviews
  - Ad-hoc phone calls
  - Contact CSM regularly for all programme enquiries
    - Support desk still first-line support route
- Broad-brush guidelines and templates to deliver
- A high degree of flexibility and CSM discretion how to manage each account

In some cases, with very large accounts, a CSM may have responsibility for one account only and will spend the vast majority of their time on customer site working in solid partnership with them to drive adoption, expansion and business outcomes.

The challenge here, for all involved, is to find a way for the CSM to feel involved with their own company and keep a balanced position and voice in the partnership. There are many stories in the world of consultancy where the entrenched consultant 'goes native' and resolutely drives for the client, even when a more balanced approach would be more valuable to achieve the joint outcomes.

Low/tech-touch
At the other end of the scale, you will have the low-touch or technology (tech.)-touch. Some companies have both. Some

companies assume tech-touch will still involve some interaction between a CSM team and the customer and so have a hybrid model.

Tech-touch in its purest form is usually implemented to serve the 'long tail' of your market; that is, the heavily populated, lower value customers. While the larger companies will provide bigger contracts and higher potential LTV, finding a way to serve the lion's share of the smaller customers in an efficient way will bring its own rewards.

There is a whole slew of products in existence now which will make it relatively easy to automate a sophisticated digital approach to engaging with your customers.

The low-touch model will also involve a limited amount of personal interaction with some or all of the accounts.

Criteria for accounts to be placed in this model would include:

- Low value, high volume segment
- Low value contracts
- Limited LTV growth potential
- Long tail accounts

Low/tech-touch usually involves

- Standard Success Plan
- Focused view on highest value product features and functions
- Assigned CSM with responsibility for large volume of accounts
  - Some companies have applied a team approach to handling this segment so contact is based on capacity

- o This can work if systems and notes are meticulously updated so the customer has a frictionless experience
- o If a customer has a number of systems to manage, their needs may be few and therefore not care if they speak to a different person each time
- o A proportion of companies I have spoken to have reverted to an assigned CSM so that the customer gets a familiar experience each time
  - There is also an argument that fewer interactions are required by the customer so they may not care or remember who they last spoke to, if they last called or emailed a year ago!
- Self-service as a first response
- Support desk as second-line response
- CSM exists as an escalation point
- Automated processes in place for
  - o Onboarding
  - o Training
  - o Driving adoption and engagement
- Surveys to drive customer understanding
  - o Automated or team call-arounds
- Annual reviews, generally held via video-conference/calls

 The ultimate challenge with this section of your portfolio is to find a way to manage them in a sustainable fashion which works for you *while also ensuring* that the customers feel part of the journey. It would be easy to alienate them through an abundance of impersonal content and a lack of personal engagement.

Medium-touch

Most conversations, presentations and workshops usually focus on either high-touch or low/tech-touch as these are the extremes, and we're in the process of finding the frameworks which can form blueprints for others.

The middle ground is just as it implies.

As an example, here is what we did as a first round of segmenting our portfolio in a more formal way and applying an engagement model to it.

To start, we reviewed our accounts and understood what we wanted our segmentation to look like, based on existing customers and our new business strategy.

Customers were put into three bands (for arguments sake, let's call them Gold, Silver, Bronze) based on their current contract value. We then allowed for anticipated growth so that we could nurture the future LTV and referrals, using the correct engagement model.

 We published these guidelines internally so that the Sales team could position CSM correctly with each of their accounts, based on current and future value.

Naturally, the Sales team would each argue the case for why their customer qualified for the highest band of CSM attention. It's important to be strict with your boundaries and monitor individual accounts over time. Otherwise, you'll end up where you started –

with the majority of your accounts in 'high-touch' and your team firefighting and overwhelmed with activities to complete.

Our second step was to look at our resources and apply a pragmatic engagement framework to each segment. For example, Gold customers would get monthly F2F meetings, Silver would get monthly calls and Bronze would get quarterly calls.

Over time, this structure was monitored in conjunction with resources and team skills and adjusted as necessary in line with the activities described in the IMPLEMENT, MEASURE and Iterate phases in this book.

Process synergies

While the engagement model names imply that only the lower tier utilises technology and automation, these are of utmost importance for each segment.

The base process should be embedded in centralised documents and templates, even if you currently don't have any automation software.

Create a process which is built around templates so that no one has to reinvent the wheel each day, hour or minute!

Your philosophy and customer journey will form the basis for your templates, your marketing team will support content creation and the product team will support with release updates and feedback processes.

The trick is to lay these foundations accessibly so that the relevant CSM can easily pick and choose the relevant tool to trigger and then spend the majority of their time undertaking value-add and relationship-maintaining conversations.

I'm sure, from the very beginning, you will have a desire to have something in place which allows you to centralise diary booking, notes and actions, exception reporting for prioritisation and triggers for red flag warnings.

This can be achieved in a spreadsheet or document; however, it soon becomes a pain point until transferred to a system designed for this purpose.

Investment in CSM technology can be a big ask in terms of both resource and finances but it's worth assessing the cost vs benefit early on in your process. Particularly for the long tail accounts, it takes away a severe pressure on general administration which can otherwise drown your CSMs.

Another trick to reducing the administration pressure on your CSMs, is to establish a CSM Operations team.

See also 1.3.1 Data! Data! Data!
              4.3 Team development

Empower and enable your teams

CSM Operations are a great way to remove the administration and framework building activities from your core CSM team. They should become responsible for the method of delivery of your programme by providing the process flow and the templates for use by your CSMs.

In turn, the CSMs should be empowered to use the parts of the process which apply to each of their customers. For example, a CSM may own a high-touch customer with whom they have a great relationship and therefore may not need to call them on a monthly basis. Conversely, a critical account may need a little more energy than the framework would usually allow.

While all customers are created equal and we want them all to be successful and shout wonderful things about us, we need to be pragmatic in the application of our resources.

Those closest to the customers will have the best instincts about each account. Trust and empower them to work how they feel will bring the best result.

Having a process allows transparency and a consistent way of working, however do not bind your team in these chains. Avoid any process which becomes a box ticking exercise rather than one which adds real value.

Choose key KPIs which empower your team rather than constrain it.

State that it's ok to choose to spend more time on a customer in a critical phase of their lifecycle and it's ok to spend less time on an account if we know we have a safety margin or we have accepted they will churn. Maybe we'll revive them in the future when we are better aligned to achieving their outcomes.

Or perhaps it's ok to hold the monthly meetings via a phone call as this is the customer's preference even though the engagement model states it must be F2F. Forcing the customer's hand in this way may be detrimental to the relationship and having a call saves travel time etc. The CSM should be able to make this call. Not only are some customers more equal than others but EVERY individual is different and that needs to be accommodated in a relationship model.

With this freedom to make operational decisions, you will enable, empower and motivate your teams.

 James Russell at Bazaarvoice explained to me that one of the biggest pain points for his Scale Team was the burden of following what they perceived to be a rigid process.

As a result of ensuring his team understood that they were empowered to make the decisions about where to spend their precious time creating the most value, their approach has changed and motivation to deliver in the right way has increased.

He feels this is a significant win in their iterative process to allow the Scale Team to make the most impact it can for their customers as well as for the business.

Close the Product gap

Earlier we talked about making the product 'sticky'. This is the art of making your product a valuable and daily habit;

something which is intuitive and compelling to use. This helps in a number of ways:

- Minimal onboarding
- Reduced investment in ongoing education and efforts to drive usage and adoption
- Increased growth opportunities as individual users become addicted to your product and refer you to their network and take your product with them when they move to their next role (this is called second order revenue)

Remember that it is important to work very closely with the Product team. If your product is making your customers successful by helping them achieve their business outcomes/ objectives, this will contribute significantly to you scaling your growth engine and your Customer Success framework.

Pioneer's round-up!

Key learnings
- ❖ Scaling describes the ability of a process or organisation to grow and manage increased demand, in a sustainable manner
- ❖ The engagement models you define will map onto the segments created for your portfolio management structure
- ❖ It is essential to consider the impact of your engagement models, particularly on the long tail/ tech-touch segment
  - ❑ We need to incorporate flexibility into the framework
  - ❑ We need to avoid alienating customers who feel shut out by the lack of personal contact
- ❖ All your engagement models will have a foundation of tech-touch delivery; there will then be layers of CSM-delivered activities in addition

Actions
- ❖ Research and consider each of the engagement models and define how they will work for you, your team, your customers and your segmentation
- ❖ Investigate and assess technology for content automation, delivery channels and the utilisation of CSM technology
- ❖ Maximise the benefit of synergies which result from using standardised processes, templates, automation and tech-touch as a foundation for all models

Hot tips

❖ A CSM Operations team will maximise the value-add activities which can be delivered by CSMs

❖ Trust your CSMs to use their judgement when it comes to using the general framework, in a flexible approach which works for them, their customer portfolio and the business

***

For more ideas and templates, download the companion workbook at www.thecspioneer.com/resources/workbook

Get in touch to share your thoughts, questions, challenges and triumphs: talk@thecspioneer.com

4.3 Team development

Whichever position you are in when you start your role in Customer Success, you are in the fastest growing profession so there are going to be lots of considerations around building your team. Everything from skills, qualities, reporting lines, compensation, securing investment and timing.

From day one, as you're designing your programme, you should be considering what the future will look like and lobbying for the investment to get to that goal

- Lobbying for funding can take time
- Budgets are generally set annually so you want to understand the timing of this and get your requirements in at the right time
- Recruitment processes can take between three to six months, longer if you're looking for a senior role
- There needs to be an onboarding and ramping up period so we're basically talking anything up to nine to twelve months from approval to productivity. Ouch!
- On the subject of onboarding, it is imperative that you prioritise onboarding your CSMs, in the same way that you would prioritise onboarding your customers. You want to set up everyone for success, your new team members, your programme, your company and your customers.

Which qualities and skills should be on the wish list for a great CSM?

There are many articles, blogs and discussions about this. People will have different opinions based on their experiences, their own career path and the debates in which they've taken part.

Characteristics of a top notch CSM

Probably anyone can be a Customer Success Manager (or whichever label you want to put on the role) with the right training, exposure and passion for any of the roles in the team. There are some fundamental skills, qualities and traits which would encapsulate a top notch CSM.

The chances are that no one CSM would be exceptional at all of these but checking for a few of the more important ones to you and the role in question will be useful during the recruitment process.

These will also support any personal development plans and career progression plans you may want to put in place, for your team

- Exudes Emotional Intelligence (EQ)
- Is a Rapport ninja
- Displays palpable passion
  - I test for passion about anything in an interview, as a starting point
  - Passion for helping people and team mates
  - Passion for finding resolutions to challenges
  - Passion for the process
- Faultless follow-through
  - Commits to actions and delivers on them
- Uses resources resourcefully!
  - Knows when, who, and how to ask for support from others
  - Doesn't overuse any resources and prioritise situations where impact will be maximised
- Business Savvy

- o Every conversation is a revenue conversation, whether it is a renewal, upsell or new business
- o We may believe that CSMs should be presented as non-commercial. However, it is important they are commercially aware in all their dealings
- Mentally resilient
  - o Days are intense, rewarding and can be draining
  - o Every conversation with a customer needs to be undertaken with the right attitude
  - o Use the support of your team to vent and maintain the resilience
  - o Supports team to create positive mental resilience
- Supremely skilled at preparation and prioritisation
  - o Time is precious, resources limited and customers are many
  - o Preparation and prioritisation will help control any lurking overwhelm and help with the mental resilience mentioned above
- Effortlessly effective communication
  - o Challenging customers' expectations and requests to ensure the right balance is maintained and partnerships remain aligned
  - o Pushing back when necessary to avoid adverse situation internally, externally and personally
  - o Clear and concise demonstration of value, achievements, responsibilities and actions
- Lush lateral thinking
  - o Quick thinking, problem resolution
  - o Raising and considering alternative solutions
- Product/Domain Expertise

○ I'm not a stickler for testing for this within a recruitment process but I will test for the passion and commitment to develop this knowledge to a trusted advisor level

Experience and background can also play a part. I have most often seen the mix of characteristics I'm after, from the Professional Services world where relationship management and passion for helping people are more highly evident. I wouldn't preclude any route into Customer Success though as it's a varied mix of skills and traits.

The most usual routes into Customer Success have been detailed as

- Customer Support
- Consulting/Professional Services
- Account Management

Equally, it will depend on the role for which you are recruiting. A more senior role for the larger accounts will need a more enhanced level of EQ (emotional intelligence) to enable the building of rapport, reading a varied number of key stakeholders and managing a complex account. For the long tail accounts, it may be more important to you to have someone who is meticulous with preparation and prioritisation.

In addition to understanding for which characteristics you're looking, the level of seniority is a key consideration during a recruitment or team structuring process. Smaller accounts, generally, may allow for recruiting less experienced staff (a couple of years out of education).

Before a period of scaling your business, it is not uncommon to segment your portfolio based on the skills that already exist in the team and assign activities accordingly.

If you want your scaling process to be sustainable, it is important to map out the segments you envisage in your future growth portfolio, the CSMs you will have dedicated to each team and then understand the attributes required for each role.

You can then appoint your existing team members in the roles which suit them best or give them a stretch objective along with a personal development plan, showing them a clear progression path. Finally, you will understand any gaps you may have in your team, the skills required and be able to proceed with recruitment armed with the right information.

 If you're not already doing this, always be on the lookout for new talent – you'll be surprised how budget can be found for a superstar, if they are ripe to be snapped up! And if the timing isn't right just now, you can keep the connection warm for a potential future partnership.

What's the magic number?

As part of the lobbying for investment, you may get asked or receive this question as push back. How many CSMs should you have to manage the portfolio?

There are a number of ways to approach this conundrum.

See also 3.3 Demonstrating Value

By demonstrating the impact you're having on revenue retention, revenue growth and the Cost of Acquiring Customers (CAC) vs CRC (Cost of Retaining Customers), you should be able to gain agreement for the investment you need to manage your portfolio.

The shape and size of your team will also be impacted by mapping the appropriate skill and seniority level to the portfolio segments. Demonstrating the skill and salary mix will help with budgetary negotiations too!

There are a few rules of thumb which are often quoted, should your management team ask for that coveted benchmarking position:

- There is an accepted rule of thumb that any portfolio would support one CSM per $2M
  - Of course, this is subject to interpretation
  - How much is the salary of one CSM?
  - Can we mix and match to the value of three CSMs if we have $6M portfolio, by having four junior roles and one senior role?
- A better approach is to understand the overall investment in Customer Success
  - Technology, Staff and Events (i.e. CRC) and set an upper and lower limit for this spending
  - Gainsight have previously published that this number should be 5%

- Resource planning based on your programme and processes
  - ○ Compelling to demonstrate the value each CSM provides and for negotiating extra resources vs revenue could lose/parts of programme to remove

Challenges

- There will never be enough people to give the level of care you feel your customers deserve or to cater for the requests for more, from them!
  - ○ Key: clear programming, segmentation, processes and use of your village
  - ○ Stick to this
  - ○ Iterate as necessary until the balance is right between the resources available to you and the positive impact on your retention rate
  - ○ Highlight opportunity cost/lost revenue of not investing in the team

CSM Operations

I cannot stress too highly, how important this team is to the success of your Customer Success programme.

A CSM Analyst was the first hire I made and this team should be responsible for providing the blueprint for every CSM to follow in their day-to-day operations.

We talked previously about finding pain points and resolving them to allow your core CSMs the freedom to add value where it is most needed.

CSM Operations are crucial in providing this support. They are responsible for all the things which drain and overwhelm a CSM who does not have this support

- Collects, analyses and reports data to help drive priorities and activities
- Defines and implements processes and systems to free up CSM time
- Creates and maintains centralised documents and templates to allow CSMs to easily effect the process
  - Creates a consistent way of working, allowing holiday/sickness cover and seamless handovers between customer contacts or exiting/onboarding CSMs
  - Removes the burden of 'reinventing the wheel' each time a CSM undertakes a routine task
  - Lifts the information gathered from notebooks to online and accessible systems
- Maintains the update of the customer journey and success programme framework

This team consists of superheroes who will help your CSMs maintain their strong and positive mental resilience and their passion for doing the right thing for the customer. The processes and systems they put in place and maintain will allow the CSMs to prepare and prioritise to maximise the impact they have on the customers' outcomes and your company's revenue growth.

When should this team make an appearance in your organisation?

My biased opinion is that the emergence of this discipline should start at the dawn of your programme. It is easy to get lost in the data and the minutiae of the portfolio when, as a CSM, you're being asked to do and be responsible for *everything* for a customer. A CSM analyst provides some focus and clarity to help you reserve your energy for the impactful actions.

Reporting line for success

We can't discuss building the team without touching on the subject of reporting line and compensation.

A much discussed and debated subject, there's enough content (as with all topics in this book) for an entire workshop and book on each!

As a headline and spoiler alert, it doesn't really matter where Customer Success (or any team) sits in the hierarchy, it is just a structure around which you conduct your business.

If the business is handling the transformation to a customer-focused philosophy skilfully, then the right motivators will be present, desired behaviours will be exhibiting and outcomes will be achieved.

 Ultimately, hierarchy is a distraction. The key to success is to ensure everyone is aligned behind the customer focus and philosophy through collaborative communication and close co-ordination.

The options for the placement of Customer Success are below

- Directly to the CEO
  - This strengthens the CS agenda and ensures a top-down approach to the company's customer focus
- Appoint a CCO

- ○ Having a dedicated Customer Success member at the C-Suite level highlights the importance of and the company's commitment to the customer focus
- Within Sales, reporting to the CRO/CSO
  - ○ This works for many, as it has all the revenue generating areas of the business in one reporting line
  - ○ As Sales is a field notoriously driven by complans (compensation plans) and rewards, having Customer Success within the same internal business function can help motivate the Sales team to care more about retention and growth from the existing portfolio
- Reporting to the COO
  - ○ This is often where Customer Success starts its journey. The skills and motivators generally witnessed in a CS team are closely linked with those of Support, Training, Professional Services and Operations teams in general

Each of the above options can and will work and many companies will, at various stages of their lifecycle, move the functions according to the prevailing business priorities and required motivators and metrics.

I repeat, the hierarchy placement shouldn't make a real difference if the company is succeeding at embedding an unconditional customer focus. In this case, every individual should be motivated and committed to doing the right thing.

In any case, defining the right metrics and compensation plans to reward the actions of everyone involved and to motivate those who may need a little nudging, never does any harm!

Metrics and compensation structures

To aid with ensuring the company maintains its focus on the right activities and outcomes, compensation plans are often used to form part of a team member's salary and benefits package.

Compensation plans are most often used in Sales environments as sales professionals tend to be heavily reward-driven, financially, and certain positive behaviours can be encouraged in this way.

Professional Services colleagues are usually compensated with a basic salary plus an element of utilisation bonus and perhaps a company level bonus based on revenue.

This mix of motivators and desired behaviours can sometimes mean that a one-size-fits-all compensation structure can be a challenge.

You will need to understand the mix of individuals you have in your team and decide how to structure your compensation package. As with everything else, you can adjust these periodically (usually annually for the apportionments but maybe monthly or quarterly for behaviour objectives).

Some considerations to have in mind include:

- A market comparable basic salary, paid monthly
- A bonus element, usually split between
  - Individual contribution to KPIs
    - Net Recurring Revenue
    - Gross Recurring Revenue

- - Upsell/Cross-sell
  - Customer Success Qualified Leads
  - Customer Satisfaction/NPS*
  - *Team contribution to KPIs*
  - An element based on % Target Revenue achieved
    - This is usually team/company-wide to align every-one on a specific goal
  - Personal development goals/objectives
- SPIFFS
  - Sales teams utilise these as additional rewards for specific competitions during a period
    - For example, the first to close a £100k deal this month will get an award of £XX, in addition to the complan commission %
  - These can be applied at short notice to drive required behaviour
    - For example, this technique could be used to drive the collecting of case studies and referrals

We know it is imperative that the entire organisation takes responsibility and understands the part they play in achieving Customer Success so that they, in turn, maximise the company's success, their team's success and finally their own success.

---

* I wouldn't recommend using customer satisfaction or NPS as a metric within a compensation plan as it could drive individuals to encourage positive feedback, and the reason for implementing such models is to gather pure and constructive feedback which will help you improve, into the future.

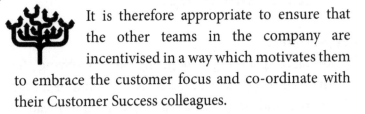 It is therefore appropriate to ensure that the other teams in the company are incentivised in a way which motivates them to embrace the customer focus and co-ordinate with their Customer Success colleagues.

An excellent way to achieve this, with incentives, is to make everyone responsible for the Customer Success headline KPI. Net Retention is a good candidate for this as it includes growth as well as retention. If this target is in everyone's compensation plan, they will do everything in their power to support this initiative.

Pioneer's round–up!

Key learnings

❖ Resource planning, budgeting and lobbying for financial investment for your team should be a high priority and be undertaken regularly and ahead of time
  ❑ Budgets are usually set annually
  ❑ Recruitment processes and onboarding to full productivity involve a significant lead time
❖ Accept that the reporting line for Customer Success will change over time; it is an arbitrary placement as the whole company should be customer and retention focused
❖ For the benefit of staff who are motivated by incentives, it is appropriate to include a component for Customer Success to highlight the priority in which the C-Suite holds this imperative
❖ CSM Operations are a key team to establish to support your team development and scaling ambitions

Actions

❖ Create a resource plan and communicate to your leadership, as an immediate priority
  ❑ Update as your plans for the team and programme develop
  ❑ Ensure this is communicated and investment committed
❖ Review your portfolio, segmentation, engagement models and existing team. Understand the skills

required and incorporate into your resource planning and recruitment process
- ❖ Research and understand the motivators for your team and company; propose a compensation plan based on your findings

Hot tips

- ❖ Skills and product knowledge can be provided through personal development plans, onboarding and ongoing training
  - ❑ Recruit for the soft skills (rapport, relationship building, EQ, etc.) which are harder to find and teach
- ❖ Hierarchy is a distraction
  - ❑ The whole organisation should have a customer focus so it shouldn't matter where you are nominally 'positioned'
- ❖ Establish your CSM Operations team as early as possible to provide consistency and clarity of activities
- ❖ Team objectives support company-wide alignment

***

For more ideas and templates, download the companion workbook at www.thecspioneer.com/resources/workbook

Get in touch to share your thoughts, questions, challenges and triumphs: talk@thecspioneer.com

Key imperatives for your journey

Customer Success has to be a philosophy first and a function second; driven and embodied from the top down.

Due to the unprecedented power of the customer, we are pioneering a strength of movement to ensure human connections and relationships bring outcomes, fulfilment and growth, both personal and professional.

While the origin story may have its foundations in SaaS, Customer Success is fast becoming and must be a business imperative for all businesses.

Partnerships and collaboration are key. We are all invested in each other's success. If we achieve our customer's desired outcomes, we will achieve our own.

Their Success = Our Success

OR

Customer Success = Company Success = Team Success = *My* Success

The company needs to be growing effectively in order to reward success internally so supporting the success of customers inherently creates your own individual success.

To grow effectively, a business would need to find two new customers for each customer which churns: one to replace the lost customer and one to drive and maintain a growth trajectory.

Create a culture of connectivity and team partnerships to drive and motivate the 'right' and natural way of working with each other and our customers.

Customer Success as a philosophy and movement is transforming the way we should do business, reinforcing age-old principles of people first and relationships. Customers are people, team mates are people, all business is about people working with people. Make your work about people. Motivate and make them successful and everything else organically grows.

Everyone in your organisation needs to be commercially aware; there is no longer a distinction between Pre and Post-Sales, every interaction with a customer is a potential sales situation.

Each customer is a joint responsibility across the organisation: *our* Account, not *my* Account. *Our* responsibility, not *your* responsibility.

The power is not held in a complex and cumbersome programme but in the simplest delivery and demonstration of *value*.

Change management is key to any adoption process. This, of course, includes your internal processes *as well as* ensuring your customers undertake a change management approach to their implementation and ongoing adoption framework. Use your trusted advisor position to ensure they understand what is needed here and help them to deliver it.

The profession of Customer Success is in a period of rapid growth and respect. The role of a Customer Success leader encompasses and requires partnerships with all areas of the business, including the revenue sustainability and growth. In part due to this, Customer Success is now becoming to be seen as *the* route to the corner office – the CEO role. So, if that's your ambition, in your own company or another, you're in a very strong position already.

Customer Success is your path to exponential growth through alignment, collaboration, partnerships, loyalty, referrals and second order revenue.

Always keep learning and having fun!

That's all, folks! For now, anyway.

I'd love to hear your thoughts on the book, your journey and have conversations with you about the future of Customer Success. Please get in touch!

Topics raised by others but not yet covered by this book:

- International organisations and teams

- Global account and CS management

- Is Customer Success a chargeable service?

- How does customer experience complement/overlap with Customer Success?

- Is outsourcing a risk or an opportunity?

Any requests for other topics to be covered in future publications? Please let me know!

talk@thecspioneer.com

Glossary

Term	Description	Text reference
Account planning	Activity often used in Sales to set priorities, win more business and schedule activities. Includes understanding expected LTV, stakeholders and key decision-makers	1.3.1 Data! Data! Data!
Advocacy	Activity that aims to influence decisions of others, i.e. promoting the benefits of using a particular product or service	1.1 Research
ARR	Annual Recurring Revenue	1.3.2 Define programme
At Risk accounts	An account which looks to be likely to cancel its contract (churn)	3.2 Customer Health
B2B	Business to Business; describes the relationship between two parties	Part I: CS is...?
B2C	Business to Consumer; describes the relationship between two parties	Part I: CS is...?
Baseline	Defining the starting point (base/basis) for measurement	3.1 Analysis & Review
Benchmark	A standard point of reference against which things may be compared	3.1 Analysis & Review
BR/EBR/QBR	Business Review / Executive Business Review / Quarterly Business Review; all terms for a periodic executive stakeholder review meeting	2.3 Roles & Resources
BYOA	Bring your own application (see also: second order revenue)	1.3.2 Define programme

Term	Description	Text reference
CAC	Cost of Acquiring a (new) Customer/Customer Acquisition Cost	Part I: CS is...?
Capital Expenditure (CapEx)	Funds spent by a business to acquire fixed assets and equipment; usually a significant sum of money	Part I: CS is...?
CCO	Chief Customer Officer	Part I: CS is...? 1.2 Foundations & Beliefs
CEO	Chief Executive Officer	1.2 Foundations & Beliefs
Ceremonial adoption	Projecting an image of being an adopter while undertaking few or none of the activities required	2.1 Commit & Communicate
Churn	When an existing customer cancels their contract or reduces their commitment to you	1.3.2 Define programme
CLTV	Customer Lifetime Value	1.3.2 Define programme
COO	Chief Operating Officer	1.2 Foundations & Beliefs
CRC	Cost of Retaining a Customer/ Customer Retention Cost	Part I: CS is...?
CRM	Customer Relationship Management. Describes the process as well as the supporting technology. Although the acronym used for the latter can also be CRMS	Part I: CS is...?
CRO/CSO	Chief Revenue Officer/Chief Sales Officer	1.2 Foundations & Beliefs
Cross-sell	To sell a different (additional) product or service to an existing customer	1.3.2 Define programme

Term	Description	Text reference
CSM	Customer Success Manager; a popular job title for someone delivering Customer Success	1.3.1 Data! Data! Data!
C-Suite	A blanket term for the team of CxOs (CEO, COO, CRO etc.) leading a business	1.3.1 Data! Data! Data!
CTO/CIO	Chief Technology Officer/ Chief Information Officer	1.2 Foundations & Beliefs
CTS	Cost to Service (a contract/ customer)	3.3 Demonstrating Value
Customer Advisory Board (CAB)	A group of customers gathered to provide feedback and advice for the future roadmap of your product/service/event/industry trends, etc.	4.1 Iterate
Customer Health	The activity undertaken to assess and understand the status of each of your customers and their likelihood to renew, grow or churn	3.2 Customer Health
Customer Health Score (CHS)	A proxy attributed to each customer, calculated on quantitative and qualitative data gathered by your organisation	3.2 Customer Health
Customer Journey	The complete sum of experiences that customers go through when interacting with your company	1.3.2 Define programme
Customer Outcomes	An initiative, goal or objective which your product/service can help them achieve	Part I: CS is...?
Customer-centric	A business focus to ensure that all dealings with your customer is undertaken in a way which provides a positive experience to drive repeat business, loyalty and referrals	Part I: CS is...?

Term	Description	Text reference
Depreciation	Reduction in the value of an asset over time; allows a business to write-off significant investments over many years, rather than taking the hit at the time of spend	Part I: CS is...?
Detractor	In NPS, a detractor will provide a score of six or less and could possibly damage your brand, service, reputation and revenue stream	3.2 Customer Health (NPS)
DIME	A framework for establishing and evolving your Customer Success function: Design Implement Measure Evolve	Part I: CS is...?
Down-sell	When an existing customer reduces their commitment to you by cancelling part of their contract with you (by reducing number of seats or number of products they take)	1.3.2 Define programme
Economic Buyer (EB)	The individual who controls the budget, makes the final financial decision and 'signs the cheque' for purchases/renewals	3.2 Customer Health
EMEA	European, Middle East and Africa. This is a geographic regional term often used for business international segmentations	
Engagement model	The approach adopted for how your team will interact with and undertake delivery of services to your customers	1.3.2 Define programme

Term	Description	Text reference
Escalations (process)	A set of procedures put in place to deal with different contexts of situations, usually involving different individuals or teams who should be notified when a specific set of circumstances exist and 'escalate' through the levels which have been defined	1.3.2 Define programme
EWS	Early Warning System; a tool which provides priorities for activities and visibility of customers who may be at risk of ending their contract with you	1.3.1 Data! Data! Data!
F2F	Face to face; usually in relation to meetings	1.3.2 Define programme
First-line support	Generally phone or internet based; it is a reactive response to incoming customer queries. It usually covers basic, generic and recurring topics. Further help can be obtained by escalating to 2nd and 3rd line support	1.3.2 Define programme
Gamification	Application of typical elements of game-playing to encourage engagement/adoption of a product or service (scores, leaderboards, rules etc.)	2.1 Commit & Communicate
Gross Retention £/% (GRR %)	The purest calculation of renewing contracts Compare value of contracts due to expire in a period with the value of those same contracts once renewed Ignore cross-sell, upsell and new business Include down-sell/churn	1.3.2 Define programme

Term	Description	Text reference
High-touch	Maintaining a high frequency and personal customer relationship	2.2 Portfolio management
KPI	Key Performance Indicator	3.3 Demonstrating Value
Lifecycle	Refers to the stages a prospect or customer experiences during their relationship with a company: Reach, Acquisition, Conversion, Retention & Loyalty	2.2 Portfolio management
Long tail	Describes the large number of customers committing to low value contracts, in contrast to the usually smaller number of customers with large contract values	4.1 Iterate
Low-touch	Involves much less personal contact and interaction; usually there is little or no interaction needed	2.2 Portfolio management
Medium-touch	A balanced engagement model between high and low-touch	2.2 Portfolio management
Mission	A short written statement of your business goals and values; What? Why? Reason for being	1.2 Foundations & Beliefs
MRR	Monthly Recurring Revenue	1.3.2 Define programme
Net Retention £/% (NRR %)	This metric includes all contract changes (not new business): Renewals, churn, upsell, cross-sell, down-sell A good metric to show overall growth of the existing portfolio Can sometimes mask a churn challenge	1.3.2 Define programme

Term	Description	Text reference
Onboarding	The process defined and followed to integrate a new customer (or employee) into the organisation, values, products and services	1.3.2 Define programme
On-premise	Hardware and software installed on the customer's premises and managed by them	Part I: CS is...?
Passive	In NPS, a passive will provide a score of 7 or 8 and could possibly damage your brand, service, reputation and revenue stream, if they are not nurtured into being a promoter	3.2 Customer Health (NPS)
Perpetual licence	Authorises the purchaser to use the software indefinitely. A maintenance contract usually accompanies this type of licence to allow the user to receive upgrades as they are released	Part I: CS is...?
Portfolio management	This is the art and science of making resourcing and delivery decisions in relation to your portfolio of customers	2.2 Portfolio management
Power of Influence	Having the ability to motivate and inspire others to take action	2.2 Portfolio management
Pre-sales (activity/ process)	Activities and interactions which take place before the customer has been formally acquired and contracts have been signed	1.1 Research
Promoter	In NPS, a promoter will provide a score of 9 or 10 and could possibly be a champion or approached for a case study/referral	3.2 Customer Health (NPS)
Prospects	Prospective customers	3.3 Demonstrating Value

Term	Description	Text reference
Proxy	An item which can be used to represent the value of something in measurement	3.2 Customer Health
QRR	Quarterly Recurring Revenue	1.3.2 Define programme
RAG	Red, Amber, Green traffic light reporting. Red = At risk/Below Target Amber = Middle ground, needs work Green = Safe/On or Above Target	3.2 Customer Health
Referrals	Directing someone to another person, in this case, for a potential customer/purchase relationship	1.1 Research
Renewal (process)	Extending the period of a contract past the existing expiry date	1.3.2 Define programme
Retention	The activities and actions undertaken to keep customers committed and under contract to your organisation (retaining customers)	1.1 Research
Roadmap (product/ service)	Maps out the vision and direction of your product/service offering into the future	1.3.2 Define programme
RoI	Return on Investment	Part I: CS is...?
SaaS	Software as a Service	Part I: CS is...?
Sales cycle	Encompasses all activities associated with closing a sale	1.1 Research

Term	Description	Text reference
Second order revenue	Revenue which comes from referrals provided by your customer portfolio, in addition to individuals changing jobs and bringing the product to their new company. This class of revenue should grow over time as the portfolio and loyalty increases due to product and Customer Success efforts	4.2 Scale Customer Success
Segmentation	Division of a broad portfolio into sub-categories (segments) based on shared characteristics	2.2 Portfolio management
SLT	Senior Leadership Team	3.3 Demonstrating Value
SPIFF	Informal term for an immediate bonus for a specific objective (new sale, certain category of new customer). It is an additional sales incentive, outside of the formal compensation plan	2.1 Commit & communicate
Sticky (product)	Finding a way to get the customer so tied to a product/service that it is difficult for them to find a reason to leave	1.1 Research
Subscription	An agreement to pay a specified amount of money, regularly as defined in the contract, for a product or service received. Usually contains minimal lock-in period	Part I: CS is...?
Tech-touch	Utilising technology to substitute human interaction, where it is possible to do so	2.2 Portfolio management

Term	Description	Text reference
Trusted Advisor	Creates a partnership with your customer based on your demonstration of having experience, training, knowledge and subject matter expertise	1.1 Research
Upsell	A customer agrees to purchase additional licences for an existing product or new products/services	1.3.2 Define programme
VC	Venture Capitalist; Investors	Part I: CS is...?
Vision	A company's roadmap identifying what they wish to become by setting a defined direction for their growth	1.2 Foundations & Beliefs
XaaS	Anything/Everything as a Service (Desktop, Platform, Infrastructure, Communications etc.)	Part I: CS is...?

Resources

A non-exhaustive list of resources! Please contact talk@ thecspioneer.com to suggest additions to the list which will be maintained online @ www.thecspioneer.com/resources-directory

The Customer Success Pioneer
- Resources @ www.thecspioneer.com
- Talk to us: talk@thecspioneer.com

ForseLucas
- Blogs and resources @ www.forselucas.com
- Training
- Consulting
- Coaching
- Mentoring

Gainsight
- Customer Success Slack Workspace
- Blogs and resources @ www.gainsight.com
- Pulse US – conference
- Pulse Europe – conference
- Pulse APAC
- Pulse Academy (Online and Live) – Training
- CCO Summit (UK and Europe)
- Book
  - *Customer Success: How Innovative Companies Are Reducing Churn and Growing Recurring Revenue,*

Nick Mehta, Dan Steinman and Lincoln Murphy, Wiley, 2016

Customer Success Association
- www.customersuccessassociation
- LinkedIn group
- SuccessCon (conference)
  - o This is a travelling series of leadership workshops
- SuccessCamp (training)

CustomerSuccessNetwork.org
- Sign up @ www.customersuccessnetwork.org to join in the conversation
- Customer Success Cafes
- Customer Success Unplugged conferences

Totango
- Customer Success Summit – conference

SaaStr
- Conference
  - o While not focused on Customer Success, it is a relevant industry as it is mostly SaaS companies at the forefront of the Customer Success movement
  - o The conference is becoming more Customer Success aware
  - o Conferences are held in the US and Europe

SaaStock
- Conference (as above)

CSM insight (Adam Joseph)
- Blogs and podcasts

Sixteen ventures (Lincoln Murphy)
- Blogs

Tri Tuns (Jason Whitehead)
- Blogs and podcasts

Cisco
- Customer Success Certification

CSM Practice (Irit Eizips)
- Blogs and podcasts

Meetups
- EventBrite and LinkedIn

About the author

Kellie has always been very passionate about people and supporting them to get the best they deserve and want to be; the best version of themselves, that they can envision.

In the early days of founding the Customer Success Network, she was named 'The Inspirer' by one of her co-founders and is a coach and mentor to friends, family, network and colleagues.

Progressing into Customer Success brought her life and career experiences into sharp focus; this was the professional movement in which Kellie was destined to play a part.

She is passionate that life is about individuals making connections and putting humanity into everything we do. We all want to be part of something meaningful. Customer Success, as a movement and philosophy, is reminding the business world at large of the best way to do business through networks and relationships.

From January 2017, Kellie spent c. 15 months in Winneba, Ghana, as Director of Challenging Heights (www. challengingheights.org). This NGO strives to work for children and youth who have been trafficked and kept in modern slavery. Children are rescued, rehabilitated and reintegrated into their community, so that they can develop into contributing and successful members of society.

Kellie continues to be driven by her passion for people, humanity and Customer Success and the need to continue supporting and initiating successful facilitation programmes across the globe.

Serving as a Trustee for Move the World (www.movetheworld. co), who use experiential education to facilitate the next generation of global citizens, Kellie is always on the lookout for similar initiatives where people are leading the change they want to see in the world.

Her mission is to support, facilitate and promote pioneers, the world over and hopes that the philosophy and passion harnessed within the Customer Success movement will be a catalyst for a greater, positive and benevolent impact on the world. Kellie absolutely believes there is a better way to do business and to comport ourselves as connected, supported global citizens.